Macmillan/McGraw

FORMS & USES OF ENERGY

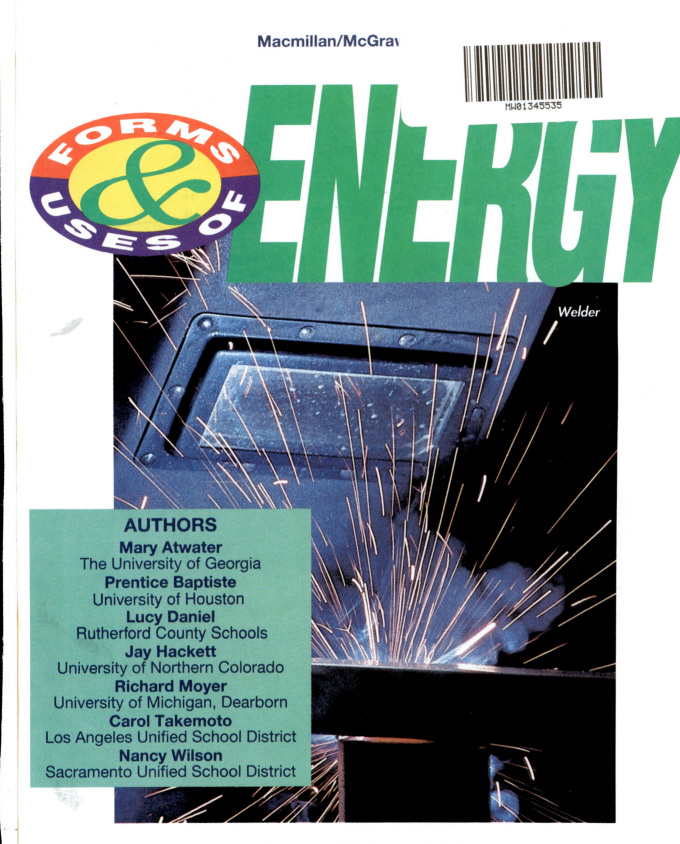

Welder

AUTHORS

Mary Atwater
The University of Georgia

Prentice Baptiste
University of Houston

Lucy Daniel
Rutherford County Schools

Jay Hackett
University of Northern Colorado

Richard Moyer
University of Michigan, Dearborn

Carol Takemoto
Los Angeles Unified School District

Nancy Wilson
Sacramento Unified School District

Macmillan/McGraw-Hill School Publishing Company
New York   Chicago   Columbus

MACMILLAN / McGRAW-HILL

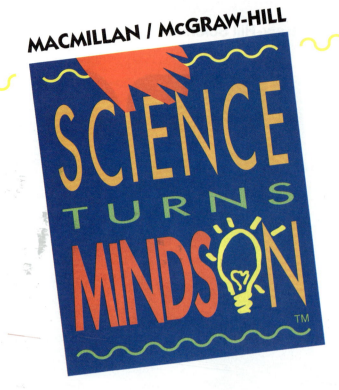

CONSULTANTS

Assessment:

Janice M. Camplin
Curriculum Coordinator, Elementary Science
Mentor, Western New York
Lake Shore Central Schools
Angola, NY

Mary Hamm
Associate Professor
Department of Elementary Education
San Francisco State University
San Francisco, CA

Cognitive Development:

Dr. Elisabeth Charron
Assistant Professor of Science Education
Montana State University
Bozeman, MT

Sue Teele
Director of Education Extension
University of California, Riverside
Riverside, CA

Cooperative Learning:

Harold Pratt
Executive Director of Curriculum
Jefferson County Public Schools
Golden, CO

Earth Science:

Thomas A. Davies
Research Scientist
The University of Texas
Austin, TX

David G. Futch
Associate Professor of Biology
San Diego State University
San Diego, CA

Dr. Shadia Rifai Habbal
Harvard-Smithsonian Center for Astrophysics
Cambridge, MA

Tom Murphree, Ph.D.
Global Systems Studies
Monterey, CA

Suzanne O'Connell
Assistant Professor
Wesleyan University
Middletown, CT

Environmental Education:

Cheryl Charles, Ph.D.
Executive Director
Project Wild
Boulder, CO

Gifted:

Sandra N. Kaplan
Associate Director, National/State Leadership
Training Institute on the Gifted/Talented
Ventura County Superintendent of Schools Office
Northridge, CA

Global Education:

M. Eugene Gilliom
Professor of Social Studies and Global Education
The Ohio State University
Columbus, OH

Merry M. Merryfield
Assistant Professor of Social Studies and Global
Education
The Ohio State University
Columbus, OH

Intermediate Specialist

Sharon L. Strating
Missouri State Teacher of the Year
Northwest Missouri State University
Marysville, MO

Life Science:

Carl D. Barrentine
Associate Professor of Biology
California State University
Bakersfield, CA

V.L. Holland
Professor and Chair, Biological Sciences
Department
California Polytechnic State University
San Luis Obispo, CA

Donald C. Lisowy
Education Specialist
New York, NY

Dan B. Walker
Associate Dean for Science Education and
Professor of Biology
San Jose State University
San Jose, CA

Literature:

Dr. Donna E. Norton
Texas A&M University
College Station, TX

Tina Thoburn, Ed.D.
President
Thoburn Educational Enterprises, Inc.
Ligonier, PA

Copyright © 1993 Macmillan/McGraw-Hill School Publishing Company

All rights reserved. No part of this book may be reproduced or transmitted in any form or by any means, electronic or mechanical, including photocopying, recording, or by any information storage and retrieval system, without permission in writing from the publisher.

Macmillan/McGraw-Hill School Division
10 Union Square East
New York, New York 10003

Printed in the United States of America

ISBN 0-02-274270-0 / 5

4 5 6 7 8 9 VHJ 99 98 97 96 95 94 93

New York City Skyline

Mathematics:

Martin L. Johnson
Professor, Mathematics Education
University of Maryland at College Park
College Park, MD

Physical Science:

Max Diem, Ph.D.
Professor of Chemistry
City University of New York, Hunter College
New York, NY

Gretchen M. Gillis
Geologist
Maxus Exploration Company
Dallas, TX

Wendell H. Potter
Associate Professor of Physics
Department of Physics
University of California, Davis
Davis, CA

Claudia K. Viehland
Educational Consultant, Chemist
Sigma Chemical Company
St. Louis, MO

Reading:

Jean Wallace Gillet
Reading Teacher
Charlottesville Public Schools
Charlottesville, VA

Charles Temple, Ph.D.
Associate Professor of Education
Hobart and William Smith Colleges
Geneva, NY

Safety:

Janice Sutkus
Program Manager: Education
National Safety Council
Chicago, IL

Science Technology and Society (STS):

William C. Kyle, Jr.
Director, School Mathematics and Science Center
Purdue University
West Lafayette, IN

Social Studies:

Mary A. McFarland
Instructional Coordinator of
Social Studies, K-12, and
Director of Staff Development
Parkway School District
St. Louis, MO

Students Acquiring English:

Mrs. Bronwyn G. Frederick, M.A.
Bilingual Teacher
Pomona Unified School District
Pomona, CA

Misconceptions:

Dr. Charles W. Anderson
Michigan State University
East Lansing, MI

Dr. Edward L. Smith
Michigan State University
East Lansing, MI

Multicultural:

Bernard L. Charles
Senior Vice President
Quality Education for Minorities Network
Washington, DC

Cheryl Willis Hudson
Graphic Designer and Publishing Consultant
Part Owner and Publisher, Just Us Books, Inc.
Orange, NJ

Paul B. Janeczko
Poet
Hebron, MA

James R. Murphy
Math Teacher
La Guardia High School
New York, NY

Ramon L. Santiago
Professor of Education and Director of ESL
Lehman College, City University of New York
Bronx, NY

Clifford E. Trafzer
Professor and Chair, Ethnic Studies
University of California, Riverside
Riverside, CA

STUDENT ACTIVITY TESTERS

Jennifer Kildow
Brooke Straub
Cassie Zistl
Betsy McKeown
Seth McLaughlin
Max Berry
Wayne Henderson

FIELD TEST TEACHERS

Sharon Ervin
San Pablo Elementary School
Jacksonville, FL

Michelle Gallaway
Indianapolis Public School #44
Indianapolis, IN

Kathryn Gallman
#7 School
Rochester, NY

Karla McBride
#44 School
Rochester, NY

Diane Pease
Leopold Elementary
Madison, WI

Kathy Perez
Martin Luther King Elementary
Jacksonville, FL

Ralph Stamler
Thoreau School
Madison, WI

Joanne Stern
Hilltop Elementary School
Glen Burnie, MD

Janet Young
Indianapolis Public School #90
Indianapolis, IN

CONTRIBUTING WRITER

Rosalyn Vu

Forms and Uses of Energy

Lessons   Themes

Unit Introduction **Forms and Uses of Energy** ...... Energy 6
How to be an investigator in science.

1 Energy Stored and Energy in Motion .... Systems and Interactions 14
Where is energy before you use it? How can you tell if something has energy?

2 What is Heat? .... Energy 26
How hot is it? How can you tell?

3 Heating Up .... Systems and Interactions 38
How do things get hot or cold? Where does the heat go?

4 Burning It Up .... Energy 50
Energy you use every day comes from very old things burned up to make heat. Where did they come from?

5 What Are Renewable Energy Sources? .... Systems and Interactions 66
What if you used something and there was more of it later? Would that be better than using it all up till it was gone?

Wrap Up **Energy at Home** .... Energy 80
Use what you know about energy to help design a place to live.

Activities!

EXPLORE

Back to You	16
Hot Stuff	28
When in Touch	40
A Hot Weightlifter	52
Wind Work	68

TRY THIS

Lights Out	10
Balloon Action	15
Where Does Energy Go?	20
Changing Energy	21
Cooling Down	31
Melt-Down	33
Scaling Up Temperature	35
Up in the Air	43
It Isn't the Matter	44
Keeping the Heat	46
Canned Heat	48
How Hard To Find?	63
Make Your Own Hot Spot	72

Features

 Links

Literature **L**inks
Science in Literature 12
Beyond the Door 56
Facts on Water, Wind and Solar Power 81

Social **S**tudies **L**inks
Early Use of Fossil Fuel 60
Towns and Energy Sources 79

Math **L**ink
Counting Calories 32

Health **L**inks
What Do Pacemakers Do? 24
Your Body's Thermostat 36

CAREERS

Energy Auditor 48

SCIENCE TECHNOLOGY AND Society

Focus on **E**nvironment
Exploring a Continent 64

Focus on **T**echnology
Energy in Focus 73

Focus on **T**echnology
Using Energy From
Not-So-Obvious Sources 77

Departments

Glossary 84
Index 87
Credits 89

Theme **T** ENERGY

Forms and Uses of Energy

Every day, all day, people around the world use energy to do things for them. **Energy** is the ability to make things move. How did you use energy today? Maybe you made your bed, cleaned your room, brushed your teeth, or walked to school. Everything you do requires energy.

People can use energy in different ways. Your body can move things. Before you pick something up or move it, you have the ability to do those things.

Energy stored in your body allows you to get out of bed in the morning, but where do your muscles get the energy to do this? Where do you get the energy that keeps your body working? Where does the energy you use come from?

When you get out of bed, you throw the covers off. The covers might knock something off the night table in the process. Moving objects have energy to make other things move, too. Energy moves from object to object just like dominoes when they knock each other down.

Sometimes you can tell energy is there by watching how it makes things move. Sometimes you know from experience that energy is stored because you know what will happen later. For example, you know a stretched rubber band will move if you let go of one end. Everything that moves uses energy. But you can't see energy. There are lots of unanswered questions about energy to explore.

Seattle, Washington waterfront

Rice farmer in Japan

Energy at work

Scientific Methods

You can't figure out some mysteries until you have enough clues. Like a detective, you see something that doesn't seem right. You think of a question or problem. Is something lost? Did someone disappear? Did something unusual happen?

Then, you think about all the possible things that might have happened. You come up with a guess about what did happen.

Actor Basil Rathbone playing Sherlock Holmes, the famous investigative detective

To prove whether you're right or wrong, you have to investigate. You may make some phone calls, talk to someone, or look in a place where the missing person or item might be. You might even make notes about each piece of information you discover in your investigation.

Finally, you decide whether your guess was right using all the information you gathered. If it's not right, you may need to find and test another possible solution to the mystery.

Scientists are very curious about the unknown. Most parts of our world are still a mystery. Every day, people are working to solve another piece of the puzzle. Science is a way of obtaining knowledge you can trust by using observation, discovery, curiosity, thought, and persistence. Scientists use many methods to solve problems. The methods they use are a lot like the ones used to solve mysteries. The steps in one simple method are:

1. State the problem.
2. Form a hypothesis.
3. Design an experiment.
4. Record and analyze data.
5. Draw conclusions.

Minds On! Write the steps of the simple scientific method described above in your *Activity Log* page 1. Now, think of a mystery you have solved. You may have found a lost shoe or figured out who ate the last cookie. Write the steps you did to solve your mystery. Beside each one write a step involved in solving a mystery. How are the two sets of steps different? How are they alike?

You use scientific methods to solve problems every day. Every time you ask a question, think of an answer, test the answer, and decide if it's right, you're thinking and acting like a scientist. You can solve an everyday problem involving energy by using a scientific method. Flashlights use stored energy to make light, but sometimes they don't work.

TRY THIS Activity!
Lights Out

A flashlight changes energy stored in batteries to produce light. If something is wrong with the flashlight, the stored energy cannot be changed. The flashlight isn't very useful then.

What You Need
flashlight, *Activity Log* page 2

Use the flashlight your teacher gives you to look into your desk or another dark place. What do you notice? What's the problem? Write your problem in your **Activity Log** in the form of a question you want to answer.

Use the steps of the scientific method to solve your problem. Make a list of the possible causes of the problem. Choose one cause that you think is the answer. Write a hypothesis that says exactly why the flashlight isn't working.

Plan an experiment of the things you will do to test your hypothesis. What things will you change? What things will you leave the same? What information will you gather in your experiment?

Test your hypothesis and write down the observations you make during your experiment. Was your hypothesis correct? Can you use your data to draw any other conclusions about your hypothesis? What should you do if your hypothesis isn't correct? What other possible hypotheses might you give? How would you follow a scientific method to test those hypotheses?

In this unit you will see more examples of how a scientific method can be used to answer questions, solve problems, and come to conclusions. You've read about the light from a flashlight. Where does the energy come from to make the light from the flashlight? How did the energy get into the flashlight? How is energy different in its various forms?

Minds On! Think about the word *energy*. In your ***Activity Log*** page 3, write a description of what you think energy is, and how you decide if something has it. Do you have energy right now? Where does it come from? If you had hot food for breakfast, how did the heat get from the burner to the pan to the food? What did you have to do to keep warm or cool on your way to school? List the kinds of energy you think exist.

Literature  Link

Science in Literature

From these books, you can learn about different and imaginative ways people have gotten and used energy. Some of the ways are not too practical, but they may give you ideas for ways that are. Since everything you do requires energy, the more ideas you discover, the more you will know about how you live and work.

Beyond The Door
by Gary L. Blackwood.
New York: Atheneum, 1991.

Scott has so much faith in logic that he's certain he will find in books the one sure explanation of everything—the single answer to what makes the universe run. In the library stacks, he finds a door that leads to Gale'tin, a sort of parallel world to Earth. He and his friend Tully become involved in a life-or-death struggle centered around a possible new energy source for Gale'tin. As you read, try to compare decisions about energy use of Gale'tin with decisions about energy use on Earth.

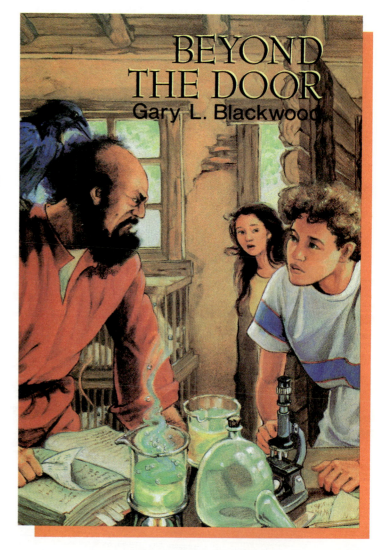

Facts on Water, Wind and Solar Power by Guy Arnold.
New York: Franklin Watts, 1990.

Most of the energy used in the world today comes from coal, gas, or oil. Unfortunately, the reserves of coal, gas and oil are being used up very quickly. However, there are large resources of sun, wind, and water energy. This book gives you information about these renewable energy sources.

Other Good Books To Read

How To Think Like a Scientist: Answering Questions by the Scientific Method
by Stephen P. Kramer
New York: Thomas Y. Cromwell Junior Books, 1987.

This book has more detailed talk about the scientific methods you can use to solve problems. Here is a question the book leaves for you to answer: Do dead snakes really cause rain?

Letting Off Steam
by Linda Jacobs.
Minneapolis: Carolrhoda Books, Inc., 1989.

Have you ever seen a geyser, hot spring, or mudpot? They are fascinating to watch. But geysers, hot springs, and mudpots are more than just fun things to watch. They are being used as alternative sources of energy in various parts of the world.

Why Doesn't the Sun Burn Out?
by Vicki Cobb.
New York: Lodestar Books, 1990.

Why doesn't the sun burn out? Why isn't the sky green or yellow? How is a wound-up spring like the top of a waterfall? This book explores energy by answering these questions and more.

Miss Pickerell Tackles the Energy Crisis
by Ellen MacGregor and Dora Pantell, illustrated by Charles Geer.
New York: McGraw-Hill Books, Inc., 1980.

To save the Square Toe County Home for Retired and Disabled Animals, Miss Pickerell needs money. She agrees to star in an antique car parade in England. But first she must track down an alternate source of energy for the cars in the parade.

Theme T: SYSTEMS and INTERACTIONS

Energy Stored and Energy in motion

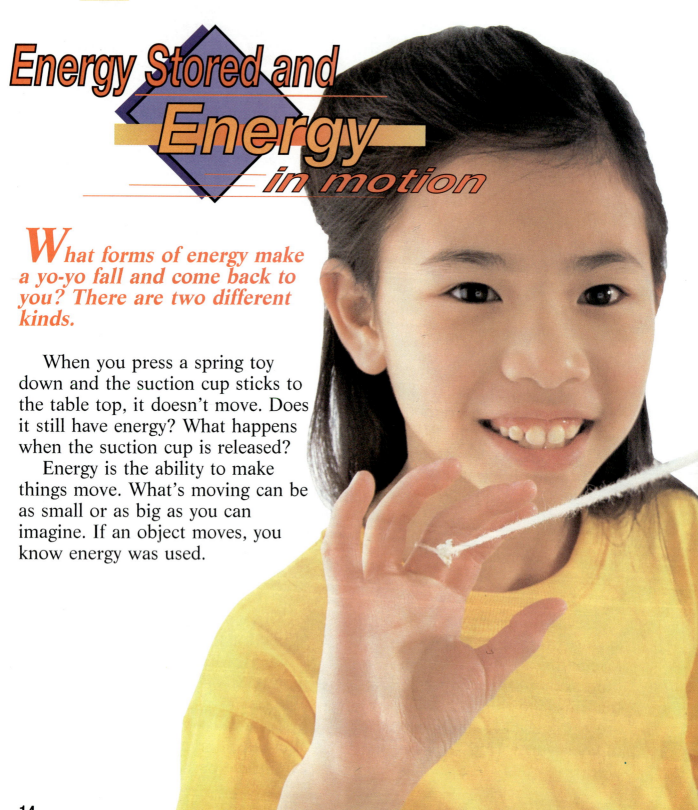

What forms of energy make a yo-yo fall and come back to you? There are two different kinds.

When you press a spring toy down and the suction cup sticks to the table top, it doesn't move. Does it still have energy? What happens when the suction cup is released?

Energy is the ability to make things move. What's moving can be as small or as big as you can imagine. If an object moves, you know energy was used.

TRY THIS Activity!   Balloon Action

How can you store energy in a balloon?

What You Need
balloon, Activity Log page 4

Lay the balloon on your desk. How would you know if the balloon had energy? In your **Activity Log** predict what will give the balloon more energy. Test your prediction. Even though an object isn't moving, it still has energy. It may have energy stored in it that can be released to make things move. How did you give the balloon stored energy?

15

EXPLORE Activity!

Back to You

How can an object change the energy it has? In the following activity, you'll make a device that uses stored energy to move. You'll see how moving things and nonmoving things can both have energy.

What You Need

books

Activity Log pages 5-6

rubber band

2 large washers

coffee can

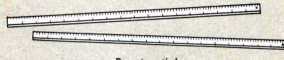

2 metersticks

What To Do

1. Cut the rubber band so that you have one long piece. Carefully thread it through the holes in the bottom of the can. **Safety Tip:** Don't touch the jagged edges around the holes.

2. Tie the washer to the rubber band.

3. Thread the rubber band through the lid of the coffee can. Tie the rubber band together at the lid.

4. Make sure the washer is twisted up in the rubber band a little before you put the lid on the coffee can.

Safety!

See the *Safety Tip* in step 1.

16

5 Predict what will happen when you roll the coffee can.

6 Roll the coffee can across the floor to your partner. What happened? Record your observations in your *Activity Log*.

7 Make a ramp with 2 metersticks and some books. The metersticks should be a few cm apart but even with each other. Line up the 50-cm mark on the 2 metersticks to check that they're even.

8 Roll the coffee can down from different heights on the meterstick ramp. Have your partner mark where the can stops and how far it rolls back. Make a chart in your *Activity Log* and record your results.

9 Predict what will make it roll back further. Use the materials to change your setup according to your hypothesis. Test your hypothesis.

What Happened?
1. What relationship did you observe between how far the coffee can rolled forward and how far it rolled back?
2. What did you observe when you rolled the can down from higher on the ramp?
3. What things did you change to make the can roll back further?

What Now?
1. Why did the coffee can roll back to you?
2. Where was the energy stored in the coffee can?
3. How was the energy released?

Kinetic and Potential Energy

The energy of the moving coffee can was stored in the rubber bands before it rolled. The energy of the moving can is called kinetic energy. **Kinetic** (ki net´ ik) **energy** is the energy of objects in motion.

The energy stored in the rubber band is called potential energy. **Potential** (pə ten´ shəl) **energy** is the energy stored in an object because of its position or its shape. The energy was stored because of the shape of the rubber band—it was twisted up and stretched.

The can rolled back when the potential energy of the twisted rubber band was transformed into kinetic energy. The distance the can rolled back depended on how hard you pushed it away or how high it started on the ramp. If you let the can continue to roll back and forth, it eventually stopped moving. The coffee can stopped rolling because its energy was changed into other forms, not because its energy was used up.

The higher the can was on the ramp, the greater its potential energy was. You gave the coffee can potential energy by lifting it up the ramp. That energy was due to the position, in this case, the height of the can.

The people carry their sleds to the top of the hill. They use the potential energy they gave themselves and the sleds when they sled back down the hill. If they only went up the hill a short way, they couldn't sled back down as far or as fast.

TRY THIS Activity!

Where Does Energy Go?

What happens to energy after you use it to make something move?

What You Need

game chips, *Activity Log* page 7

The chips symbolize all of the energy resources of the universe. Each student represents a different form of energy. Count all of the chips in the class and count how many you have. Write both numbers down in your **Activity Log**.

Follow your teacher's directions to transfer chips to your classmates. Count how many chips you have when you're done. Count the total number of chips in the class again. Has there been a change? Which number changed? What conclusions can you make about the total amount of energy in the universe?

Energy is never created or destroyed, it only changes form. In the Try This Activity, the chips only changed hands. There was always the same number of chips. In the Explore Activity, the energy of the can wasn't used up. It was transformed to other kinds of energy—sound and heat. The can made noise as it moved and transferred energy to the air and your ears.

The tires of the racing car move fast against the pavement before they grab and the car moves. The movement produces friction and the tires get hot enough to smoke and burn.

Friction slowed the can down when it rubbed on the floor and the metersticks. Friction is also at work when your hands are cold and you rub them together. The kinetic energy from the rubbing changes into heat energy and your hands warm up. The friction slowed and stopped the can because it transformed the can's kinetic energy into heat.

Chemical Potential Energy

When you lifted the coffee can in the Explore Activity, you used potential energy stored in your body. **Chemical (kem´ i kəl) energy** is a form of potential energy stored in matter when atoms join together to form chemical compounds. It can be released when matter undergoes a chemical change. You get your chemical potential energy from the food you eat. Do the Try This Activity below to see a common example of chemical energy.

Gasoline has chemical potential energy. The energy is released when the gasoline burns in a car's engine. The energy is used to make the car move.

A flashlight battery has chemical potential energy that is transformed to electric energy when the battery is connected in a circuit.

TRY THIS Activity!

Changing Energy

What kind of energy puffs up biscuits and cookies?

What You Need
plastic spoon, 1 level spoonful of baking soda, goggles, 4 spoonfuls of vinegar, paper, funnel, 1-L bottle, balloon, *Activity Log* page 7

Safety Tip: Vinegar is an acid. Baking soda is like salt and can sting and burn in cuts and scrapes. Use goggles.

Put on your goggles. Using the funnel, put the vinegar in the 1-L bottle. Make a paper funnel and use it to put the baking soda inside the balloon. Being careful not to drop any baking soda in the bottle, put the balloon neck around the bottle neck. Now, lift the balloon up and shake the baking soda down into the vinegar. Describe in your **Activity Log** what happened. Was energy released? How can you tell?

Keeping the Beat

Many machines we use control the transformation between potential and kinetic energy. We use those machines to do work for us. A grandfather clock has a spring that is wound up, just like the rubber band in your coffee can. As the spring unwinds, it changes its potential energy to the kinetic energy of the moving pendulum. The clock keeps the correct time because the pendulum moves back and forth regularly. The clock wouldn't work well if the pendulum didn't swing back and forth in a regular pattern.

A tiny catch, controlled by the regular swing of the pendulum, lets the clock spring unwind bit by bit, not all at once or in spurts. Without the pendulum, the spring, and the tiny catch, the clock would not work.

How Doctors Help the Beat Go On

Sometimes a person's heart can be like a grandfather clock with a faulty control. The chemical energy stored in the heart muscle is not released in the right pattern and the heart beats irregularly. It doesn't contract and move blood through the body as it should.

A person with an irregular heartbeat may become dizzy because his or her brain doesn't get enough oxygen-carrying blood. Or, blood may collect in parts of the body long enough to form dangerous blood clots.

When the irregular beat is bad enough to be dangerous and can't be controlled with medicine, it's necessary for doctors to implant a small, battery-powered machine in the patient's chest. The machine, called a **pacemaker**, is connected to the heart muscle. The chemical potential energy of the batteries is transformed to electric energy. The machine sends small, regular shocks into the heart to keep its beat regular.

Another operation is required to replace the batteries when they wear out.

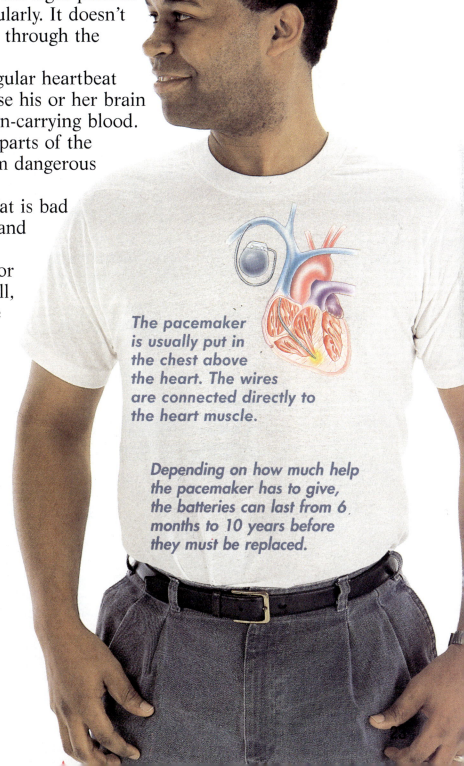

The pacemaker is usually put in the chest above the heart. The wires are connected directly to the heart muscle.

Depending on how much help the pacemaker has to give, the batteries can last from 6 months to 10 years before they must be replaced.

Health  Link

What Do Pacemakers Do?

You'll need a tape recorder, a cassette, a pencil, a clock with a second hand, two partners, and your *Activity Log* page 8.

Put the tape in the recorder. Turn on the recorder and press *play* and *record*. Tap on or near the microphone every few seconds. Don't watch the clock or count to yourself. Put 10 taps on the tape, then let your partners do the same. Then, say "stop" into the microphone. Now, fast forward the tape a few seconds. Have a partner watch the clock and touch you lightly every 5 seconds. When they touch you, tap on or near the microphone. Tap 10 times, then switch positions until everyone has tapped. Stop, rewind the tape, and listen to your taps. In your *Activity Log* describe how your partner was like a pacemaker.

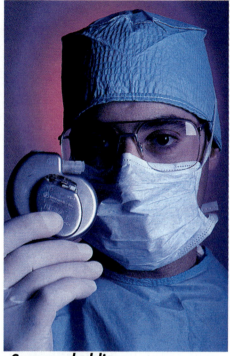

Surgeon holding a pacemaker

Sum It Up

Minds On! Look at the description of energy that you wrote in your **Activity Log** on page 3. Would you change it now? Name and describe some different types of energy on page 8 of your **Activity Log**. Compare your answers with those of your classmates.

Something as simple as a yo-yo wouldn't work if energy didn't exist. The kinetic energy of its movement couldn't be stored. That stored energy couldn't be used to make the yo-yo wind back up the string. Something as complex as your body wouldn't work if chemical potential energy stopped changing to kinetic energy inside your body. You couldn't use the chemical potential energy of the food you eat to carry out many activities, like walking, and bicycling. Kinetic and potential energy affect every part of your life.

Critical Thinking

1. Does a helium balloon have potential energy? How can you tell?
2. If you had a waterfall behind your house, how could you use the kinetic energy of the falling water to make other things move? Would this be useful for you?
3. Describe the energy changes that occur when you are swinging in a swing.

25

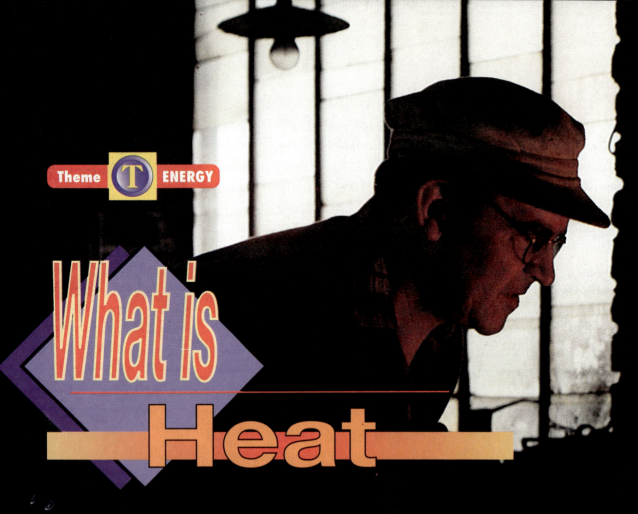

Theme T ENERGY

What is Heat

***W**hen it's cold out, you can warm yourself by standing in the sunshine or moving close to a fire. You won't get rid of a chill standing in the shade or moving away from a fire. What kind of energy is making you warm?*

When you sit down to eat a meal, some of the different foods on your plate are usually hot. As you eat, some cool down faster than others. Why does this happen? Where does the heat go?

If you are eating an ice cream cone, you probably don't leave the ice cream sitting around for very long. You know it will melt because of the heat. Why doesn't the ice cream stay cold?

Minds On! Imagine you're a blacksmith like the one in this picture. How many horseshoes could you cool off before all the water boiled away? Would it happen faster if the horseshoes were the same temperature, but bigger? How could you find out?

EXPLORE Activity!

Hot Stuff

How "hot" are things that are the same temperature? This activity will help you understand how "hotness" is really measured.

What You Need

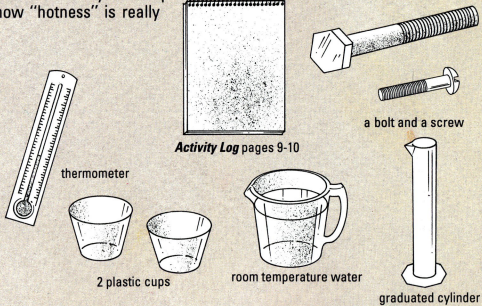

Activity Log pages 9-10

a bolt and a screw

thermometer

2 plastic cups

room temperature water

graduated cylinder

What To Do

1. Observe the difference in size and weight of the bolt and screw.

2. Carefully measure 20 mL of room-temperature water into your 2 cups. Measure the temperature of the water in each cup with the thermometer. Record the measurements in your *Activity Log*. The temperature of the water in each of the cups must be the same when you start.

3 Your teacher will put the bolt and screw in boiling water for a few minutes. Then, your teacher will place a bolt into 1 of your cups of room-temperature water.

4 As soon as your teacher places the bolt in the cup, take the temperature of the water in the cup. Record the temperature in your *Activity Log*. Take the temperature of the water in the cup every 15 s until it reaches room temperature again. Record the water temperatures in your *Activity Log*.

5 Use the other cup of water and repeat steps 3 and 4 for the screw.

What Happened?

1. What was the temperature of the bolt and screw when your teacher removed them from the boiling water?
2. What happened to the water in each cup?
3. What were the highest and lowest temperatures for each cup?

What Now?

1. Why was the highest temperature of the water in the two cups different?
2. Make a graph in your *Activity Log* of your data showing the temperature changing over time. How are the shapes of the graphs similar? How are they different?
3. Predict the results for a third, more massive bolt or screw.

EXPLORE

What Is Temperature?

The bolt and screw that your teacher placed in your cups were the same temperature. They were all in the same boiling water. Your two cups of water also started at the same temperature. But after the bolt and screw were placed in the cups of water, the water did not warm to the same temperature. The more massive bolt heated the water to a higher temperature than the smaller screw.

You measured the temperature of the water with a thermometer. Air temperature is measured with a thermometer too, but how does a thermometer measure temperature? Air is made of atoms and molecules of gases. Those atoms and molecules are moving around. Because they have mass and are moving, they have kinetic energy. We perceive that energy as temperature, hot or cold.

You may think that all atoms are always moving at the same rate, but they're not. There are always some that are moving faster than others. The average kinetic energy of the millions of faster and slower atoms of air is their **temperature**.

The sides of the pool table will be hit by many pool balls. Measuring the energy of each ball and finding an average energy would be like taking their temperature.

A thermometer is hit by millions of atoms. Each atom may give or take a little energy when it hits the thermometer. The thermometer measures their average kinetic energy.

What Is Thermal Energy?

In the Explore Activity, the only difference between the bolt and screw was their mass. They were both made of the same thing. They both were heated to the same temperature. Do the Try This Activity to see how mass influences cooling.

Thermal (thûr´ məl) **energy** is the total energy of particles in matter. When there is more matter at the same temperature, then there is more energy. For instance, the bolt in the Explore Activity had more mass. It had more thermal energy, even though it was the same temperature as the smaller screw.

TRY THIS Activity!

Cooling Down

Does the amount of thermal energy control cooling?

What You Need
125 mL of warm water, graduated cylinder, 2 cups, thermometer, *Activity Log* page 11

Pour 100 mL of warm tap water in one cup and 25 mL of warm tap water in another cup. Take the temperature of the water in each of the cups. Record your measurements in your *Activity Log*. Which cup has a greater amount of water? Which of the cups do you think will reach room temperature first? Why? Record in your *Activity Log* the temperature of the water in each cup every minute as they cool to test your prediction.

Hot soup becomes room temperature when you leave it out for a while. A cup of soup will cool quicker than a whole pot full. The soup heats the air in the room, but because there's so much air, you don't notice the room getting just a little warmer as the soup cools.

What Is Heat?

Heat is thermal energy moving from a warmer object to a cooler object. Heat always flows from the warmer to the cooler object—never the other way around. You never expect to stand in front of a fire and get cool!

Heat is measured in calories. A **calorie** (kal´ ə rē) is the amount of thermal energy it takes to raise the temperature of one gram of water 1°C. It would take 500 calories to warm 500 grams of water from 20°C to 21°C.

Your body changes some of the food you eat to thermal energy. The thermal energy provided by food is measured in Calories. It's confusing, but food Calories are bigger than calories. One food Calorie is the same as 1,000 "regular" calories. We use food Calories because ordinary calories are too small to conveniently measure the energy in the food we eat.

Thermal energy is moving from the hot flame to the beaker of water. You would never expect the beaker to give thermal energy to the flame and make the flame hotter.

Math Link

Counting Calories

How much thermal energy would it take to make a cup of hot tea? If you had 200 grams of water at room temperature, about 20°C, how many calories would it take to heat the water to 80°C? Use your calculator to get the answer. Describe in your *Activity Log* on page 12 how you solved the problem.

If it took 500 calories to raise the temperature of a mass of water from 20°C to 40°C, how much water was there? Use a calculator to get the answer.

If you've ever used an ice chest, or cooler, you probably know you don't need to worry about the temperature in the cooler as long as there is ice inside. Why do you suppose that is? Do the Try This Activity and you'll see why.

Once the water got cold, it stayed the same temperature until all the ice melted. You found out that thermal energy from the water, your hands, and the surrounding air melted the ice. Only when all the ice was melted could all the water start to get warmer. This is true for water boiling in a pan, too. The temperature of the boiling water stays the same until all the water is boiled away. If you let a pan of water boil dry on the stove, the pan will get very hot and probably be damaged.

TRY THIS Activity!

Melt Down

What is the temperature of water with melting ice in it?

What You Need
1/2 cupful of water, several small pieces of ice, spoon, thermometer, **Activity Log** page 13

Put the ice in the cup of water. Have your partner stir the water with the spoon while you hold the cup in your hands. Measure the temperature of the water every minute until 5 mins after all the ice melts. In your **Activity Log** graph how the temperature of the water changes over time. How does the temperature change?

The cooking noodles won't burn when there's water in the pan. Energy from the burner goes to boil the water and cook the noodles. The pan doesn't get any hotter than the temperature of boiling water until all the water is gone.

Measuring Temperature

Cooks use a meat thermometer to tell when meat is done and a candy thermometer when they make fudge. You know how to read a thermometer to tell how hot or cold it is outside. A nurse has probably taken your temperature with a fever thermometer when you've been sick. The types of thermometers you've seen all depend on the regular expansion and contraction of liquids or solids because of temperature changes.

How Does a Thermometer Work?

In 1714, Gabriel Daniel Fahrenheit (far′ən hīt′) (1686–1736), a German physicist, developed a thermometer that worked like those we use today. Fahrenheit's thermometer measured the expansion and contraction of mercury in a closed tube. Mercury is a shiny, metallic element that is a liquid at room temperature. It is very useful for thermometers because it expands and contracts a lot for a very small change in temperature. This makes it much easier to measure a small change in temperature.

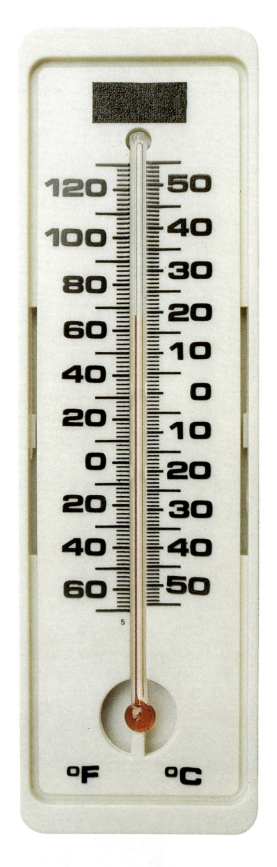

Fahrenheit's scale was based on the number of degrees in a straight angle, 180. The temperatures for freezing and boiling were the markers at each end of the scale. The temperature of an ice and salt water (brine) solution was 0°F and the temperature of the human body was 98°F. Using this scale, ice melted at 32°F and water boiled at 212°F (32°+180°).

34

Twenty-eight years later, Anders Celsius (sel′ sē əs) (1701–1744), a Swedish astronomer, developed a metric temperature scale. His scale had only 100 degrees between the temperatures for freezing and boiling water. The original scale read backwards. Look at the photograph and compare the Fahrenheit and Celsius scales.

Using the original Celsius scale, the boiling point of water was 0°C and freezing was 100°C. On today's Celsius scale, average human body temperature is 37° and a comfortable room temperature is 20–22°.

Activity!
Scaling Up Temperature

TRY THIS

What do you have to do to make a working thermometer?

What You Need
1-L glass bottle, clear drinking straw, colored water, clay, marker, dropper, ice water, Activity Log page 14

Fill the bottle almost to the top with colored water. Insert the straw and seal it in the bottle with clay. Leave about 3/4 of the straw sticking out of the bottle. Use the dropper to add colored water to the straw until it is about 1/2 full. Wait a few minutes for the bottle of water to reach room temperature. Mark the water line on the straw. Now, put the bottle in a container of ice and water. Wait until the water line stops moving. Mark the water line. What should the temperature of the ice water be? What temperature is the thermometer measuring? In your **Activity Log** describe the steps you would follow to mark your thermometer so it corresponds to the Celsius scale.

Thermostats

Often, it's important to control the temperature of our surroundings. A device that controls temperature by opening or closing a switch is called a **thermostat** (thûr′ mə stat′). If your home or school has air conditioning or heating, it is turned on and off by a thermostat. Ovens and some electric appliances like irons also use thermostats to keep them at a certain temperature.

The inside of a thermostat

The coil of metal unwinds when it gets hot and winds up when it gets cold. The winding tilts the glass capsule. The liquid inside the capsule moves between the wires and closes the circuit. The circuit turns the heat on or off.

Health Link

Your Body's Thermostat

Your body has a thermostat, too. It controls how you use the energy in food to keep you warm. When you're healthy, your body temperature stays very close to 37°C (98.6°F). There are special sensor cells in your brain that balance things that cool you off, like sweating, with things that warm you up, like exercise and how much food is converted to thermal energy. This balancing act between heating up and cooling down is called **homeostasis** (hō′ mē ō stā′ sis).

When you have a fever, the sensors in your brain are confused by the bacteria or viruses causing the illness. The delicate balance of homeostasis is disturbed.

Use a fever thermometer to take the temperature of all your classmates. Are all the temperatures close to 37°C? What are the highest and lowest temperature? What is the average of the whole class?

Sum It Up

Because we use thermal energy to cook food and keep us warm, it's important to be able to measure temperature and heat accurately. You'd be very uncomfortable in the winter if a heater made rooms 40°C (104°F) instead of 20°C (68°F). Can you imagine what would happen if ovens couldn't be controlled and they burned all the food put in them? Understanding how this form of kinetic energy, thermal energy, transfers from warmer objects to cooler objects and having an accurate scale to measure that energy change are useful. They allow us to use thermal energy more effectively.

Critical Thinking

1. What different kinds of thermometers have you seen? Is there a connection between what they're used for and how accurate they are?

2. What are some ways that you have stored heat to be used later?

3. You've felt cold, warm, and hot water. Once water freezes, can it get even colder? How?

Theme T — SYSTEMS and INTERACTIONS

Heating Up

Heat travels on its own. Sometimes we want it to go places, and sometimes we don't.

Minds On! Imagine you have a round blob of "heat" in your hands that you need to get to a friend across the room. In your *Activity Log* on page 15 describe ways you could get the heat blob to your friend. What's different about the ways you thought of? What's the same?

A vacuum bottle does a good job of keeping hot drinks hot and cold drinks cold. The outside isn't hot or cold to the touch. Why don't you feel the temperature of the drinks inside of the bottle?

Bright sunshine makes you warm. The sun also provides much of the energy on Earth. Between Earth and the sun are millions of kilometers of vacuum. How does the warmth of the sun reach Earth?

In the next activity, you'll explore one way thermal energy gets from place to place. If you like to eat, pay attention. This way of energy transfer has a lot to do with cooking.

EXPLORE Activity!

When in Touch

How does thermal energy move from one object to another when the two objects are touching?

What You Need

Cool tap water

very hot water

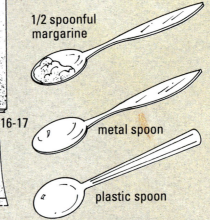
1/2 spoonful margarine

metal spoon

plastic spoon

Activity Log pages 16-17

aluminum foil   2 plastic cups   paper towel

What To Do

1. Stick half the margarine to the middle of the handle of each spoon. Put the spoons in the cups to check that the margarine piece barely sticks out over the side of the cup. Remove the spoons from the cups.

2. Predict which spoon will melt the margarine faster when they are put into the hot water.

40

3 Fill a cup with hot water and put the spoons in. Watch the margarine. What happens? Record your observations in your **Activity Log**.

4 Feel the ends of the 2 spoons. Is there a difference in temperature? Record your observations in your **Activity Log**.

5 Cool both spoons by placing them in a container of cool tap water for a few seconds.

6 Cover the plastic spoon with aluminum foil. Predict which spoon will carry the heat faster now. Test your prediction.

What Happened?
1. Which spoon got heat to the margarine faster?
2. What effect did the aluminum foil have on how the spoon got heat to the margarine?

What Now?
1. Why did margarine on the spoon handle melt?
2. What can you say about what the spoons were made of and how well the heat traveled?
3. In your **Activity Log**, sketch where you think the heat moved in the activity.
4. What effect do you think covering the metal spoon with foil would have?

Looking Ahead
You'll use the same materials for the next two activities to learn two more methods of heat movement.

Conduction

In the Explore Activity, the margarine melted on the handle of the spoon because thermal energy was transferred from atom to atom in the spoon. The transfer of thermal energy from atom to atom in solids is called **conduction** (kən duk´ shən). Most metals are good conductors of thermal energy. Conduction is like handing your blob of heat to the closest person then to the next closest person.

Cooking pans are made out of metals that conduct heat well, like aluminum, copper, or cast iron. If the pans weren't made of good conductors, they'd have hot spots because the thermal energy wouldn't travel quickly to all parts of the pan. Part of the food would burn and part wouldn't cook at all. The next Try This Activity will show you another type of thermal energy transfer connected to cooking.

Cooking uses conduction to transfer thermal energy. Thermal energy is conducted from the burner to the pan, then from the pan to the food.

The thermal energy from the flame is being conducted through the metal bar to the beaker. The thermal energy is boiling the water.

TRY THIS Activity!

Up in the Air

How does heat move through the air?

What You Need
2 cups, metal spoon, plastic spoon, very hot water, margarine, **Activity Log** page 18

Fill a cup with hot water. Put an equal amount of margarine in the bowl of each spoon. Hold both spoons close over the hot water at equal distances, but do not touch the water. What happens? Discard the margarine into the empty cup. Record your observations in your **Activity Log**. Hold your hand over the hot water, but do not touch the water. What do you feel? Record your observations in your **Activity Log**. Write down one way you can use this information.

Convection

In the Try This Activity, the margarine melted, but the spoon wasn't touching the water. Thermal energy must have traveled in a way different from conduction in this activity. The margarine melted because the water heated the air above it. The hotter air was less dense. Denser, cooler air around the cup pushed the lighter, warmer air upward toward the spoon. The hot air rose and warmed the spoon and the margarine melted.

The transfer of thermal energy by the movement of heated liquids and gases is called **convection** (kən vek´ shən). Convection is like carrying the blob of heat across the room to your friend. If you picked this way of thermal energy transfer, you'd be like the atoms and molecules of warm air carrying the thermal energy from the warm water to the spoon.

Convection also uses matter to transfer heat. Most of the bread you've ever eaten was baked in an oven that used convection. The bread pan doesn't actually touch a burner, like on a stove top. The bread sits in the middle of the oven. The air heated by the oven burner rises past the loaf pan.

TRY THIS Activity!

It Isn't the Matter

How does heat move when there's no matter to transfer it?

What You Need
2 cups, metal spoon, plastic spoon, very hot water, margarine, *Activity Log* page 19

Make sure the spoons are room temperature. Fill a cup with hot water. Put equal amounts of margarine into the spoons and hold the bowls of the spoons near, but do not touch, the outside of the cup. What happens? Discard the margarine in the empty cup. Record your observations in your **Activity Log**. Hold your hand near the outside of the cup, but do not touch it. What do you feel? Record your observations in your *Activity Log*.

Radiation (rā′ dē ā′ shən) is a way of transferring energy that does not require matter.

If you decided to just throw your blob of heat to your friend, you picked a method like radiation. Only the thermal energy traveled. There was no matter (you or your classmates) between the source of energy and where it ended up.

Radiation

In the Try This Activity, the spoons and your hand weren't touching the cup or water and they weren't above the hot water. The thermal energy you felt when you held your hand beside the cup couldn't have gotten there by conduction or convection. The thermal energy was being transferred by radiation.

Even though your hand felt warmth, there probably wasn't enough thermal energy transferred to melt the margarine. Radiation doesn't work as well as conduction and convection for transferring thermal energy at these temperatures. That's why vacuum bottles work so well. The glass (or stainless steel) vacuum bottle doesn't conduct thermal energy very well. The bottle is closed at the top, so convection can't transfer thermal energy away either.

Energy from the sun moves to Earth by radiation. There is almost no matter between Earth and the sun. It's almost like Earth is outside a vacuum bottle and the sun is the hot drink on the inside. Only because the sun is so hot do we feel its warmth here on Earth.

The thermal energy that makes you feel warm when you stand in the sun travels from the sun through a vacuum by radiation. Thermal energy from the sun causes weather on Earth.

Controlling Thermal Energy Transfer

As you saw in the Explore Activity, some substances conduct thermal energy better than others. However, sometimes good conduction isn't what you want. Remember the vacuum bottle? Some cooking pans have wooden handles for the same reason—to keep them cool. We usually want to control how hot or cold things get. Knowing more about how different materials transfer thermal energy can help us do that. In the Try This Activity below you can find out which materials control thermal energy transfer.

TRY THIS Activity!

Keeping the Heat

What can you use to control how fast heat moves? You'll test materials to see how much they slow the transfer of thermal energy.

What You Need
various materials, 1 jar with lid, thermometer, tape, very hot water, *Activity Log* page 20

Predict which material you think will best keep the hot water from losing thermal energy. Now, in your **Activity Log** design and draw a way to use one of the materials provided to keep the water from losing its thermal energy. Prepare a jar according to your plan. Plan to read the thermometer on the inside when your jar is ready. When everyone is ready, your teacher will add 300 mL of water to all the jars. Record the temperature of the water in your jar and in the plain jar your teacher has. After 20 min., record the temperature in each jar again. In your **Activity Log** draw a graph to show how the temperature of the water changed in each jar. Compare your results with your classmates. Which jar showed the least temperature change? Which showed the most? Why?

Materials that do not conduct thermal energy well are called **insulators** (in´ sə lā´ tərz). Air, wood, newspaper, and wool are all fairly good insulators. Insulators usually contain trapped air spaces. Air itself is a fairly poor conductor of thermal energy. However, convection can transfer thermal energy quite well in air. When the air is trapped in tiny pockets, convection currents can't act to transfer thermal energy.

The air pockets trapped in this fiberglass insulation prevent convection currents from transferring thermal energy. The fiberglass itself is a poor conductor of thermal energy.

Insulation helps keep buildings warm or cool. Insulation is usually placed in the walls and ceilings of homes. It helps reduce the cost of heating and cooling the home. The cost savings is also a savings in energy resources. For many reasons it's important to conserve valuable energy resources.

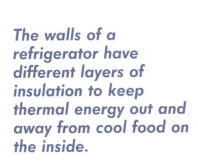

The walls of a refrigerator have different layers of insulation to keep thermal energy out and away from cool food on the inside.

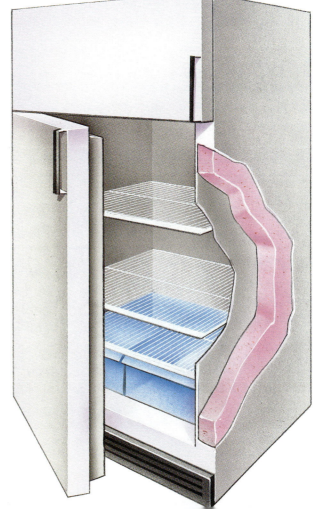

Careers

Energy Auditor

Madeleine Xavier is an energy auditor. She needs to know how thermal energy is transferred from place to place. She visits homes, offices, and factories. During her visit she goes through a checklist and measures how energy is being lost or wasted in a building. When she has completed the checklist and measurements, she suggests ways to use less energy to heat, cool, and light the building. She may suggest adding more insulation, using more efficient appliances and lights, and installing different heating or air conditioning systems.

Differences in thermal energy conduction are important for insulation. How substances absorb and radiate heat can also be important. Do you think color has anything to do with the way objects absorb or radiate energy? Do the Try This Activity to find out.

TRY THIS Activity!

Canned Heat

Can dark colors make you warmer?

What You Need

black can (inside and outside), silver can (inside and outside), cool tap water, warm tap water, thermometer, *Activity Log* page 21

Fill both cans with cool tap water and measure their temperatures. Record the results in your *Activity Log*. Set the cans in a sunny window and measure their temperature after 20–30 min. Record the temperatures in your *Activity Log*. Fill the cans with hot water and measure their temperatures. Set them in the shade to cool. In your *Activity Log* predict which can will cool quicker. Test your prediction after 20–30 min and record the results in your *Activity Log*. How does color affect how objects heat up and cool down?

Heat is absorbed differently by different-colored objects. The black can heated up faster because the dark color absorbed more heat than the light color. It also cooled faster because black radiates thermal energy more efficiently. This is why cooking pot handles are often black, pizza boxes are usually white, and solar heat panels are black. Without looking, can you guess what color car radiators are?

Sum It Up

Thermal energy is transferred among objects by three methods—conduction, convection, and radiation. Understanding how thermal energy moves helps us keep heat where we need it. By understanding heat we can make pans that get hot with handles that stay cool. By using materials that are poor conductors, we can prevent heat transfer. Learning how to control heat transfer can save money and energy resources.

Insulated clothing

Critical Thinking

1. Where are the heat vents or radiators located in your home? Is this a good or bad location? Explain why.

2. How can you apply the information about how colors affect heat absorption to choosing clothing colors for different kinds of weather?

3. Think about two houses with the same amount of floor space. One house has all of its rooms on one floor, while the other house has two stories. In which house is there likely to be more heat loss?

Burning It Up

Theme T — ENERGY

How does a car use the energy in gasoline to make motion? You already know part of the answer because you know how thermometers are affected by temperature.

At least part of the electricity you've already used today came from coal or oil. How does a power plant use the chemical potential energy in coal or oil to make electricity? Because so much of the electricity used comes from coal and oil, finding new sources is as important as finding new ways to use less coal and oil.

You may know that coal comes from mines and oil comes from wells. But do you know how coal and oil were made and how energy is stored in them? Coal and oil are being made right now, but you may be surprised to find out when they'll be ready to use.

Minds On!
Imagine you need to lift something big. You have all the tools you need, but your only source of energy to do the work is thermal energy. Think of everything you know about thermal energy, how it travels and how it affects matter. Brainstorm with a partner and sketch or write your solution in your *Activity Log* on page 22.

EXPLORE Activity!

A Hot Weightlifter

Gabriel Daniel Fahrenheit used expanding and contracting mercury to measure temperature. Can expanding and contracting air also be used to do work?

What You Need

What To Do

1 Cut the neck off the balloon.

2 Stretch the balloon tight over the top of the tall jar. Make sure the balloon is centered over the jar top.

3 Put tape around the neck of the jar to hold the balloon in place.

4 Place the fork face up on top of the balloon with the points just over the edge of the jar top. The bowl of the fork should be at about the center of the balloon. Now, tape the fork to the edge of the jar so the tape acts like a hinge.

5 Put the balloon jar as far as possible into a 16 oz. jar half full of cold water and hold it there. What happens to the end of the fork? Record your observations in your *Activity Log.*

6 Now, put the balloon jar into a 16 oz. jar half full of hot tap water as far as possible and hold it there. What happens to the end of the fork? Record your observations in your *Activity Log.*

7 Use some string and tape to see how many washers the fork and jar can lift.

What Happened?
1. What happened to the air in the jar when you chilled it?
2. What happened to the air in the jar when you warmed it?
3. How many washers could your jar lift?

What Now?
1. How could you make your jar lift more washers?
2. Think about what you know about water heating on the stove. Would the jar and fork work as well if the jar was completely full of water instead of air?
3. What would happen if you actually boiled water on the inside of the jar?

EXPLORE

Making Things Move With Thermal Energy

The jar in the Explore Activity used thermal energy to make the fork move. The air in the jar expanded when it was heated and contracted when it was cooled. The jar changed this expansion and contraction to an up-and-down motion of the fork.

The way materials react to changes in temperature is the source of motion for many machines you're familiar with. In a car, gasoline burns rapidly inside the cylinders of the engine. The up-and-down motion of pistons in the cylinders is transformed to the forward motion of the car.

In a car engine, the gas burns, releasing hot gases that expand rapidly in the cylinders. The gases push the pistons down. The hot gases are forced out to the car exhaust through valves when the pistons are moved up again.

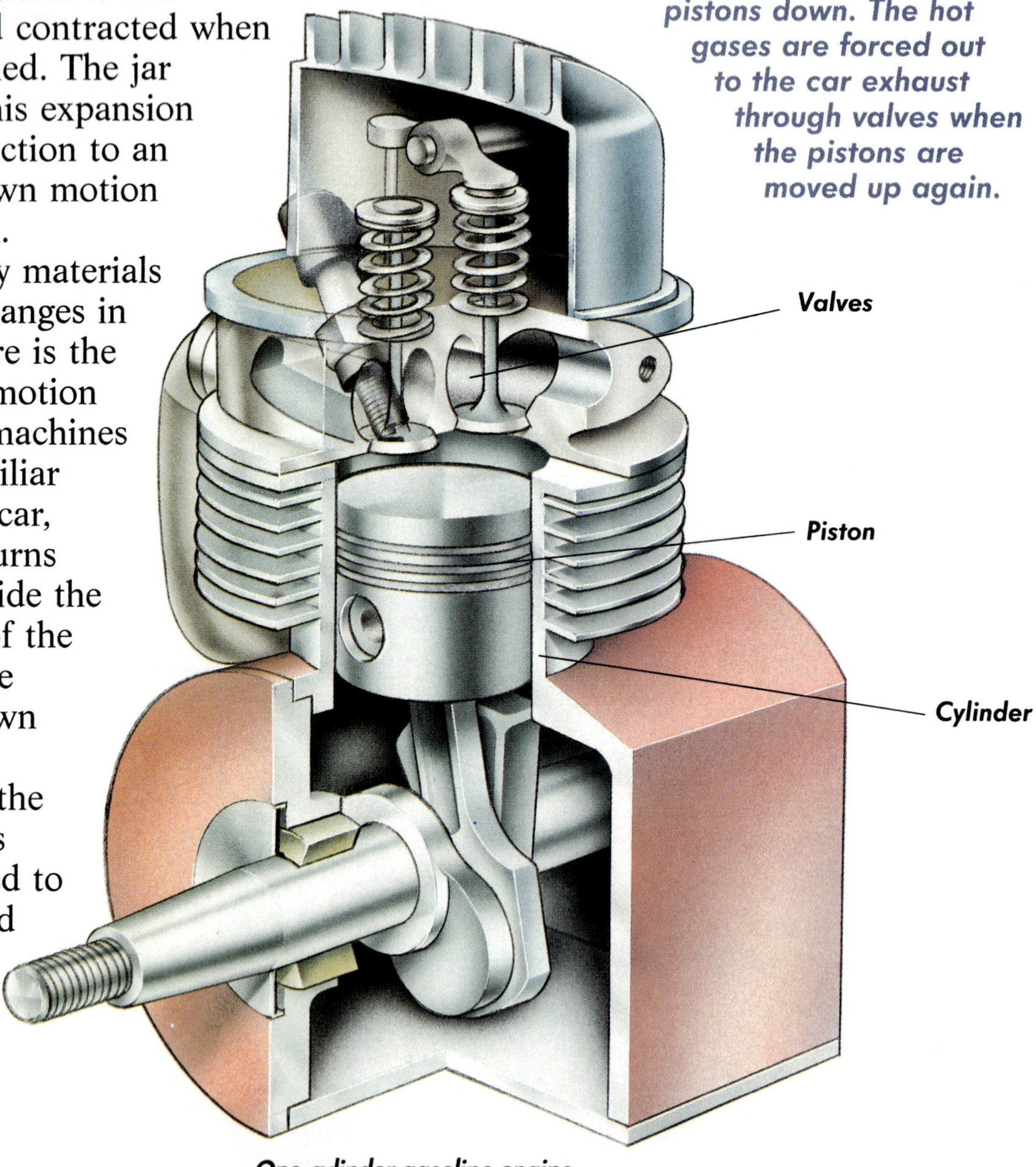

- Valves
- Piston
- Cylinder

One-cylinder gasoline engine

The chemical potential energy in the gasoline changes to the mechanical energy of pistons in the car. **Mechanical** (mi kan′i kəl) **energy** is the energy of moving objects.

The first steam engines were also like the jar and fork in the Explore Activity. These engines burned wood or coal that heated water to make steam. The steam was used to make pistons move in cylinders. The energy of the moving pistons was used to drive machinery. Old locomotive trains and some early cars used steam engines.

Internal view of steam engine

Steam pushes the piston back and forth and turns the wheel.

Steam inlet

Slide valve

Exhaust

Piston rod

Cylinder

Piston

In early steam engines, the hot, expanding steam was piped into one side of a cylinder. As the steam expanded, it pushed a piston. While the steam expanded, it was cooled by surrounding metal and cooling pipes. The cooled steam was piped out as hot steam was let into the other side of the cylinder.

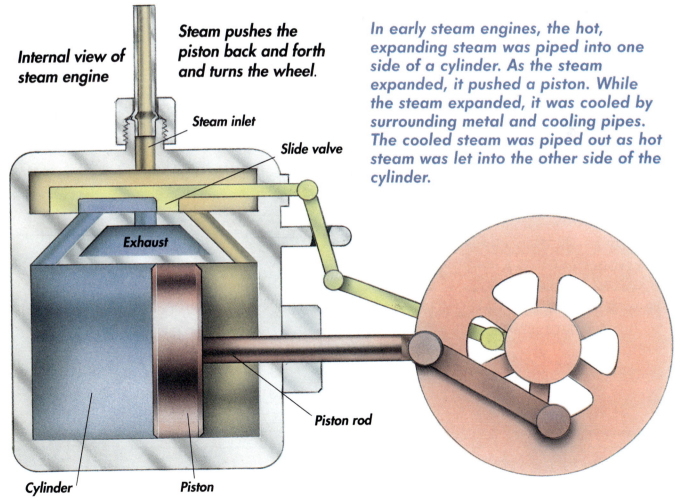

During the 1800s, steam engines changed the way people did work. Factories sprang up where coal, wood, and water were plentiful. They used the energy from coal or wood to do work, such as weaving or metalworking, on a large scale. Because the products of steam-driven factories took less time and labor to make, they cost less.

Literature  Link

Beyond the Door

Steam power can be used to do many things. In the parallel world Gale'tin of *Beyond the Door*, Tomeas is trying to get the people of the valley to accept a new source of energy. He wants to use a mineral, soarite, to make steam and run factories. Scott and Tully are in the middle of the dispute between Tomeas and the valley people. As you read the story, keep a list of what would have to change for it to have a happy ending for everyone involved. Then, re-write the story to have a happier ending.

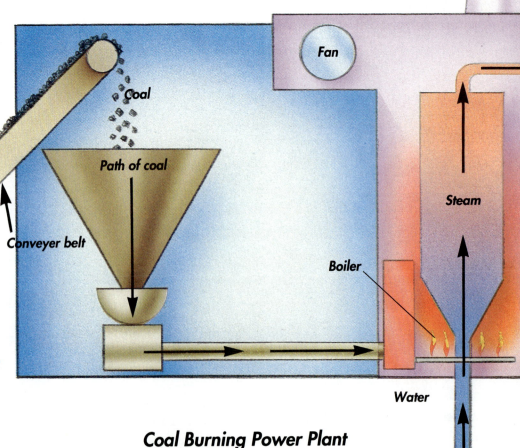

This modern generating station burns coal to make electricity.

Coal Burning Power Plant

56

We're still getting things done with steam today. Many modern generating plants burn coal or oil to make steam. Like the expanding air in the Explore Activity, the kinetic energy of rapidly expanding steam is turned into something useful—electricity.

Many different kinds of energy interact to make the electricity that you use every day. Chemical potential energy from coal is transformed to kinetic energy to make electricity. **Electric** (i lek′ trik) **energy** is a form of kinetic energy—the energy of moving electrons.

You use electricity to cool food, cook food, operate computers, communicate with others, and thousands of other things. You change electric energy to other forms when you use it to make heat, light, or motion.

Turbines (tûr′ bīnz) are giant fans with many blades. Steam passing through makes them turn just like wind makes a fan or pinwheel turn. Spinning turbines turn generators to produce electric energy.

Minds On! What have you used electric energy for today? What use are you making of electric energy right now? Make a chart in your **Activity Log** on page 25 that shows what the electricity did and what forms of energy it was transformed into. •

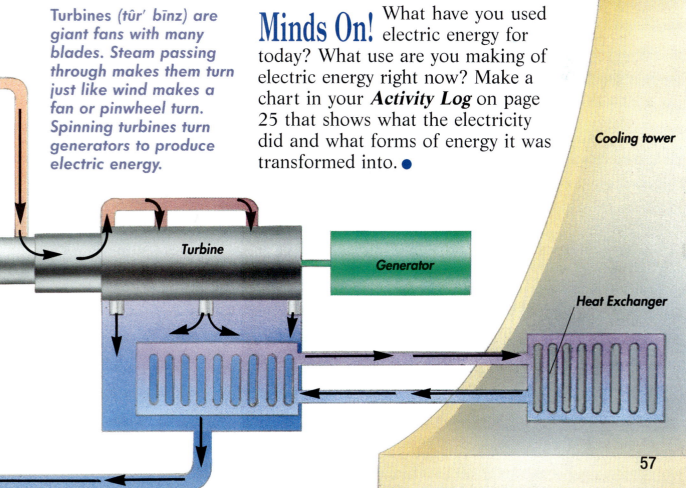

57

Where Do Coal and Oil Come From?

The chemical potential energy in coal, oil, and natural gas is often used to make electricity. That potential energy came from the sun. Coal, oil, and natural gas are called **fossil fuels** because they formed from the remains of plants and animals that lived on Earth millions of years ago. While they were alive, the plants and animals stored chemical potential energy.

Fossil fuels are a nonrenewable energy source. **Nonrenewable** energy sources are those that can't be replaced by natural means in less than 30 years. It took millions of years to make a supply of these fuels, and it will take millions to make another supply. Fossil fuels only exist in areas that used to be seas or swamps millions of years ago.

When oil is fresh out of the ground, it's a thick, smelly, black fluid. It is separated using heat and chemicals to make gasoline, chemicals, and other fuels.

1. *Petroleum, or oil, and natural gas were formed from the remains of prehistoric animals, plants, and small organisms that settled on the ocean floor.*

2. *Over millions of years, these organic remains were buried. The heat deep inside Earth and pressure of the overlying rock caused chemical changes in the organic material to form oil and natural gas.*

Formation of Oil

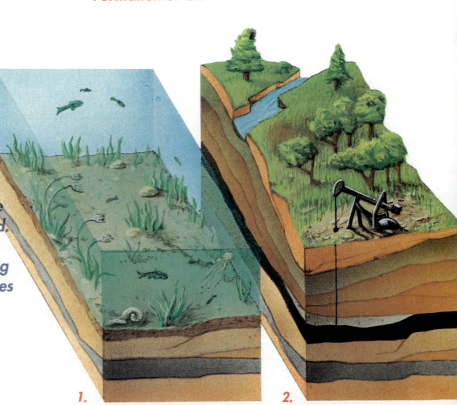

1.

2.

Oil is used for other things besides a source of energy. It is refined to make gasoline and other products. For example, oil is burned in a special chemical reactor to make carbon powder. This black powder is required to make car tires and some other plastics—things you probably use every day.

Natural gas is colorless and odorless. The utility company adds an odor so people will notice leaks and unlit burners. Natural gas is most often used as a source of thermal energy in gas stoves, furnaces, and water heaters. Because it costs less to heat with natural gas, many people use it instead of electricity.

Coal is most often used as a source of thermal energy for power plants. It's also an important part of refining iron ore so it can be used to make things.

Coal is a dark, black mineral with shiny parts.

Formation of Coal

1. Coal formed from the remains of plants that grew in swampy areas as long as 300 million years ago.

2. Heat and pressure caused chemical changes in the plants to form coal.

Social Studies Link

Early Use of Fossil Fuels

You may think fossil fuels have only been used in the last few hundred years, but the Chinese found natural gas more than 2,000 years ago. They drilled holes hundreds of feet into the ground in search of salt and discovered natural gas. They used the gas to heat and light their homes, and prepare food. The Chinese also found oil in the same salt wells that produced natural gas.

You are now aware of many uses and advantages of fossil fuels. However, every source of energy has drawbacks. Make a list of the advantages of fossil fuels. Work with a small group of classmates and research the disadvantages of using fossil fuels. Try to find as many disadvantages as advantages. In your group, decide how good or bad burning fossil fuels is. Then, make a presentation to the class to convince them of your choice.

Drawing of salt drilling derrick from around 100 B.C.

Energy From Atoms

Fossil fuels aren't the only nonrenewable energy source. The potential energy stored in the nucleus, or center, of atoms is called **nuclear** (nü´ klē ər) **energy**. Some elements can be made to release nuclear energy. These elements are not fossil fuels, but they are nonrenewable energy sources. The supply of them is limited. They are getting harder to find, just as fossil fuels are.

When the center of an atom, the nucleus, of certain elements is split, energy is released.

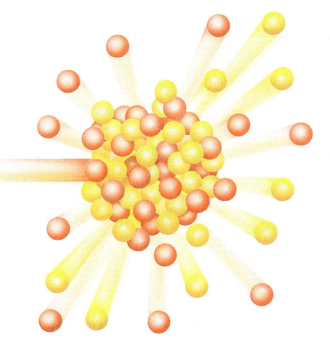

It doesn't cost much to run nuclear generating plants, but building them is very expensive. The waste from nuclear power plants can be dangerous for hundreds or thousands of years. Because the waste is dangerous, it must be stored safely. The safety of operating nuclear power plants is always a concern. A 1986 accident at a nuclear power plant in Chernobyl (châr no´ bəl) in the former U.S.S.R. took many lives. The results continue to endanger a great many other lives.

There are benefits and costs for every source of energy. Both nuclear energy and fossil fuels produce waste when they are used. The more we use them, the more we pollute. It is important to balance the dangers of pollution and waste with the benefits of energy.

The energy released from splitting atoms is mostly in the form of thermal energy. The thermal energy is used to boil water and produce steam to make electricity.

Atomic Electric Plant

The Importance of Conservation

Minds On! What would happen if you were stuck in your home and all the food you had there right now was all the food you could have for a month? How would your eating habits change? In your *Activity Log* page 26, make suggestions of the ways you could limit the amount of food wasted in your home.

Oil, natural gas, and coal are nonrenewable fuels. Because it takes so long for coal, oil, and natural gas to form, when people use them, they are gone forever.

Although we haven't discovered all the sources of fossil fuels on Earth, finding them is becoming more difficult as sources are used. Searching for new sources and developing them is expensive.

Consumption of fossil fuels worldwide has been increasing every year. Recently, the rate of increase has slowed. However, the amount of coal, oil, and natural gas remaining to be used continues to shrink rapidly.

TRY THIS Activity!

How Hard To Find?

Which resources are used up first and why are remaining resources harder to find?

What You Need
25 chips, clock with a second hand, *Activity Log* **page 27**

Have 1 person in your group hide the 25 chips in your group's area of the room. Allow 1 person in the group 15 s to find as many of the chips as possible. Record the number found in your *Activity Log*. Allow a second person to search for 15 s, then a third. Record in your *Activity Log* the number of chips found. Who found the most chips? Why was it easier for the first person than the third to find the chips? Were all the chips found? What reasons can you give for this? How is this related to shrinking fossil fuel resources?

In the Try This Activity, it was easier to find chips when there were more available. The easy-to-find chips were found and "used up" first. Your work became more difficult and took longer when many of the chips were gone. If you had to have a certain number of chips, you would have to conserve and stockpile energy sources during plentiful periods. You might also have to do without when the sources were harder to find and earlier sources had been used up.

Other Costs of Fossil Fuels

Many possible sources of fossil fuels are in wilderness areas. Some coal deposits lie under national parks. Many possible sites for off-shore oil drilling are near coastal wildlife refuges that oil spills could damage. When the Alaskan oil pipeline was being planned, many argued that it would damage the surrounding plants and animals.

In addition to pollution, the loss of beautiful wilderness areas may become a cost of fossil fuels. As coal, oil, and natural gas become harder to find, people are beginning to consider mining and drilling in wilderness areas. Do you think they should? What would make it necessary?

Focus on Environment

Exploring a Continent

At the southernmost part of the world is Antarctica, the seventh continent. It was sighted in 1820, but first explored in the early 1900s. In the last 30 or so years, more than 15 countries have sent teams to explore Antarctica.

Researchers have studied much of Antarctica and how it is related to the rest of the world. They have discovered that fossil fuel and mineral sources are buried on the continent.

More than 38 countries have signed a treaty giving up territorial claims to Antarctica and reserving it for peaceful scientific research. Environmentalists are concerned about the effect researchers may have on Antarctica. They're also afraid that countries who haven't signed the

treaty may want to mine the fossil fuel resources there. Some people would prefer to see all Antarctic exploration and development carefully monitored.

Work with a group of classmates and research the possible effect of research and development on Antarctica's environment. Do you think there are enough reasons to mine Antarctica for fossil fuels? Why or why not?

Antarctica

Sum It Up

We get energy from burning fossil fuels and splitting atoms. Because we use that energy to run machines, we can do work without using our own muscles. Can you imagine how much trouble it would be if you had to use your muscles to wind up a big spring to run a school bus? However, we seem to need more and more energy as we find new ways to use it. The costs and benefits of energy sources must be studied in order to make wise choices for the future.

Critical Thinking

1. How could you use the heat from burning coal to make something move?
2. Would you ever expect to find fossil fuels on another planet? Why or why not?
3. Much of the Middle East is dry now and there are plentiful oil resources deep under the soil. What must the area there have been like millions of years ago? How do you know?

Theme **T** SYSTEMS and INTERACTIONS

What are Renewable Energy Sources?

When fossil fuel sources become too difficult or costly to find, how will we heat and cool our homes? Very old sources of energy are being used in new ways to solve this problem.

A modern windmill used to generate electricity

How do you think people made light and kept warm before they discovered coal, natural gas, and oil? How did they get from one place to another? How did they run machines? As fossil fuel sources are used up, people are rediscovering these early energy sources and finding new uses for them.

These energy sources will play an important role in providing energy in your future. Some of them are so common you can find ways to get and use the energy from them yourself.

An old windmill used to grind grain and make flour

Minds On! Imagine you can't burn any gasoline or diesel fuel to get home from school today. Is there anything besides muscles that you could use to get you there? ●

EXPLORE Activity!

Wind Work

You may have used the wind for fun when flying a kite. The energy of the wind can also be used to do more practical things. Could you use the wind near where you live to do work?

What You Need

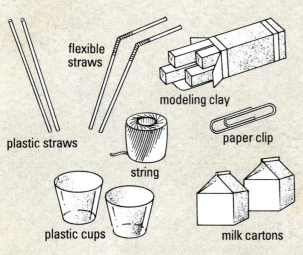

flexible straws, plastic straws, modeling clay, string, paper clip, plastic cups, milk cartons

construction paper, paper fan, Activity Log pages 28–29, toothpicks, tape, glue, cardboard, scissors

What To Do

1. In your **Activity Log**, draw a plan for a device that can use the wind's energy to pick up paper clips.

2. Predict how many paper clips your device can pick up.

3 Use the materials provided to build your machine.

4 Test your device at different wind speeds.

5 Revise at least 1 part of your device so that it will work better.

What Happened?

1. How many paper clips did your device pick up when you first built it?
2. How well did it work at different wind speeds?
3. How did you "connect" the wind to the paper clips you were trying to pick up?

What Now?

1. What improvement did you try to make your device work better?
2. Why is using wind energy less convenient than using electricity to do work?
3. Why might it be important to test windmill designs before they're built?
4. Wind speed can vary a lot. How can you control the work your windmill does at different speeds?

Renewable Energy Sources

In the Explore Activity, you designed and built your own windmill, your own machine for using the energy of wind to do work. You considered the characteristics of the wind you needed to harness, the work you needed it to do, and the materials you had available to build it.

Wind is just one renewable energy source.

Renewable (ri nü´ ə bəl) energy sources can be replaced by natural means in less than 30 years. Other renewable sources of energy include moving water, the energy inside Earth, once-living matter, and the sun. Just as there are advantages and disadvantages to using fossil fuel, there are good and bad results from using renewable energy sources, too.

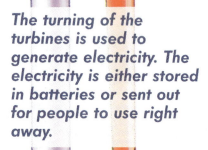

Modern wind turbines are windmills used to produce electricity. They may measure up to 100 meters (about 330 feet) across and are computer-programmed to get the most energy from the wind.

The turning of the turbines is used to generate electricity. The electricity is either stored in batteries or sent out for people to use right away.

Energy From the Wind

Remember how convection transferred thermal energy in gases and liquids? Winds and all of our weather develop from the convection currents caused by the uneven heating and cooling of Earth's atmosphere.

Wind is actually a form of solar energy. When the sun heats the atmosphere, convection currents of warm air rise and colder air moves in below. We feel the moving air as wind.

Humans have used the energy of wind to do work for hundreds of years. They used wind to grind grain and to sail ships. The Persians (Iranians) were using wind machines over 1,300 years ago to grind grain. There are still windmills grinding grain and pumping water today.

A large windmill farm

To make the best use of wind, turbines must be built in areas where the wind blows most of the time at 12 or more kilometers (about 7 miles) per hour. Because the wind doesn't blow all the time, storing energy to use during less windy times can be a problem. More than 90 percent of the land suitable for using wind energy is concentrated in the western United States from Texas to Montana.

A large, wind-generator farm located near Palm Springs, California produces about one percent of the state's electricity. The wind is a very economical energy source for that part of California. To get that electric energy another way you'd have to burn almost three million barrels of oil.

There is almost no pollution from wind energy. However, some argue that large, wind-generator farms mar the beauty of the landscape. Wind-generator farms are expensive to build, but the price of wind energy is becoming competitive with coal, oil, and natural gas.

Energy From the Sun

The sun is the primary source for almost all of Earth's energy. There appears to be no end to the supply. The sun's energy creates virtually no pollution on Earth. Ultraviolet (UV) light from the sun is dangerous, however. If you've ever had a bad sunburn, you know some of the damage UV light can do. People don't usually think of sunlight as pollution, though.

Each day, the amount of energy the United States receives from the sun is equivalent to the energy from 22 million barrels of oil. However, to try to capture all that radiant energy, the entire country would have to be covered with collectors. You can make a collector to catch a small part of that radiant energy. Do the Try This Activity to find out how.

Each mirror at the solar generating station is about a meter square. The mirrors follow the sun throughout the day and focus its rays on pipes that carry a synthetic oil that stores thermal energy.

TRY THIS Activity!

Make Your Own Hot Spot

What can you do to concentrate energy from the sun?

What You Need
various materials, 2 thermometers, *Activity Log* page 30

Design and build a solar collector using available materials. Remember what you know about thermal energy. Be sure 1 thermometer is inside and shaded by your collector when you build it. Set your finished collector outside in the sun. Put the other thermometer in the shade near the collector. In your **Activity Log** record the temperature inside and outside the collector every 10 min for the next 40 min. Graph the temperatures on a line graph. Compare your results with those of your classmates. What relationship was there between the materials used and the temperature rise inside the collector?

Solar energy is most often used to heat water or homes. Roof-top water heaters and windows that face the sun are the most common solar collectors. Sunlight can also be used to make electricity. Solar-powered calculators use small solar cells to do this. However, calculators only use a small amount of electricity. Converting large amounts of solar energy directly to electricity is expensive and inefficient.

Solar furnace in France

View of many solar collectors at solar-energy-power generating station in San Bernardino, California

Focus on Technology

Energy in Focus

At one station in California's desert, a million mirrors are catching the sun's energy to generate electricity. The thermal energy from the sun is collected and used to boil water. The steam from the water turns turbines to generate electricity.

When sunlight is most intense, air conditioners are working their hardest. Solar energy provides extra electricity when it's most needed, during the hottest part of the day. It's expensive to buy and build solar-energy-powered generators. However, once you buy the equipment, getting and using the energy doesn't cost much. In the end, solar energy can cost less than other sources.

Energy From Water

Water wheels have been used to capture the kinetic energy of falling or flowing water since 100 B.C. Water wheels are simple machines that are turned by flowing water. Today, the energy of moving water is often used to make electricity. Electricity generated by falling or flowing water is called **hydroelectric** (hī′ drō ə lek′ trik) power.

The energy from falling water comes from the sun. The water cycle depends on evaporation. Water from the ocean is evaporated by the sun's heat. Clouds form and carry the water over land. The water falls as rain. The sun is what "lifts" the water up behind the dam.

Hydroelectric plants at dams don't produce any pollution. However, dams do change the land around them. When they're built, the people and animals living where the lake will be must move. All the trees under the lake die and the environment of the area changes.

Some possible sites for dams are located in wilderness areas. There is concern about upsetting the ecology of these regions. Because most dam sites are far from populated areas and industrial centers, long wires must be installed to carry the electricity generated to where it can be used.

To get a source of water falling from a great height, dams are built. Turbines are installed at the base. Water falls down from the lake through the turbines to generate electricity.

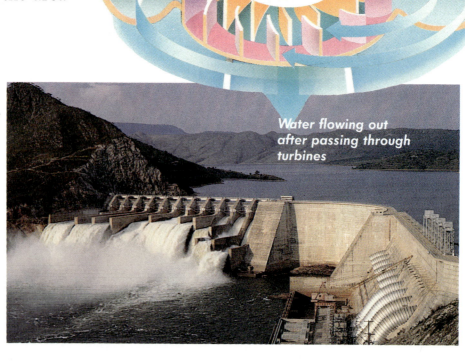

Water flowing out after passing through turbines

Energy From Tides

The ocean's tides can generate electric energy in much the same way that hydroelectric power is produced from running water. The rising tidewater flows through turbines to generate electricity. When the water level falls, the water flows out through the turbines.

Tide generators work best where there is a big difference in water level between high and low tide. This limits the number of places turbines can be built to use this energy. Most places that would be good sites for tide-powered generators are far from population centers. They would require installation of long wires to transport the electricity generated.

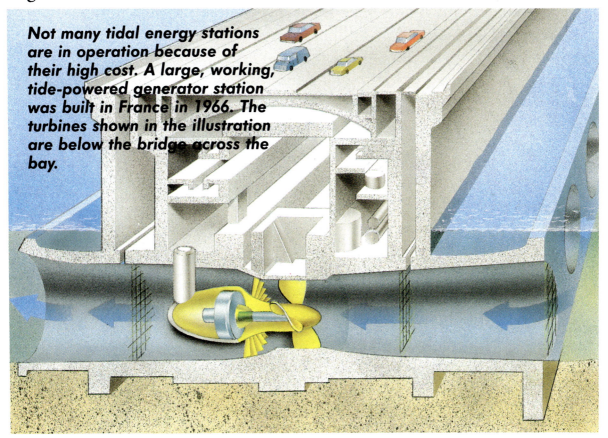

Not many tidal energy stations are in operation because of their high cost. A large, working, tide-powered generator station was built in France in 1966. The turbines shown in the illustration are below the bridge across the bay.

Tidal generators produce little pollution. However, they change the flow of water in the environment where they're constructed. Many plants and animals living in the harbors and river mouths would be affected by tide-powered generator stations.

Energy From Inside Earth

Because science has helped us learn more about Earth, we now have a more complete explanation of geysers and hot springs. Water under Earth's surface passes over very hot rock that heats it. When steam pressure builds up, the steam and water escape through Earth's surface. The steam and heat can be used to heat buildings and generate electricity. This energy from Earth is called geothermal energy. **Geothermal** (jē′ ō thûrm′ əl) **energy** means *Earth-heat* energy.

There aren't many easy-to-use sources of geothermal energy. In areas where geothermal energy is available, like Iceland and New Zealand, it's a cheap and relatively pollution-free energy source.

Scientists and engineers are trying to get geothermal energy where they want it by drilling wells five to six kilometers (over three miles) deep and pumping water deep into Earth's crust to be heated. They plan to use the heat they extract from the crust to boil water, turn turbines, and generate electricity.

You've probably seen pictures or heard of geysers or hot springs and the steam and hot water that flow from them. Native Americans who believed Earth was alive, might have explained geysers as Earth breathing. Can you see how they might have viewed geysers as breaths, belches, and burps?

Biomass

Biomass (bī′ ō mas′) is any matter that is or was living. Remember how fossil fuels were formed from dead plants and animals? Biomass could be thought of as the early stage of coal. You can burn biomass or products of biomass to get thermal energy. More than fifty percent by weight of landfill waste is paper, cardboard, and yard wastes. These can all be burned for thermal energy. Animal and human manure are other waste products that can be dried and burned.

In some areas, products from biomass are burned. Alcohol produced from biomass is burned and used to run cars in Brazil. Brazil is trying to use alcohol in more cars to reduce pollution and their dependence on expensive, imported fossil fuels. Heat and a gas called methane are produced when biomass decomposes. The heat and gas can also be used.

Burning biomass can produce less of some kinds of pollution than burning fossil fuels. However, you must burn much more biomass than coal to make the same amount of electricity. This makes biomass more expensive to use because so much more of it has to be transported.

 Focus on Technology

Using Energy From Not-so-obvious Sources

Dairy farmers in Tillamook, Oregon are looking for the best use for 1.6 million kilograms (3.6 million pounds) of water used to wash livestock and a use for 900 thousand kilograms (2 million pounds) of manure produced each day on their farms. Manure can be used as fertilizer. However, its use results in odor and health problems. It could also be burned for energy, but building a plant to do so would be expensive. How could they use the manure? What else would you need to know to decide?

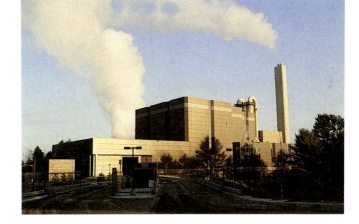

Trash-burning power generating plant

Energy and Where You Live

Fossil fuels have been used for hundreds of years to provide light and heat for homes. Other sources have been used for much longer. Having other energy sources available to do work is very important to how you live. Many of the sources you've learned about in this unit depend on climate or location.

Hong Kong, Bombay, Boston, Chicago, London, San Diego, and Lisbon all have one thing in common. They are cities built near oceans, lakes, or rivers. In the past, water provided cheap transportation and a source of energy for producing food and building materials. Inland cities, like Dallas, Texas, are more likely to have started near major roads or railroad lines.

Sources of energy are important for making and using the things people need to live and work, and for transportation. In the past, towns were built near forests or easy-to-get coal.

What sources of energy have been used in your town in the past? What sources are still being used today? The energy of moving water may have been used for transportation or making things. Remember water wheels and mills? Your town or city may have started near a source of wood (biomass). Solar energy for growing crops may have played a part, too.

Social Studies Link

Towns and Energy Sources

Find out more about the history of your town or city. See if you can discover what renewable energy sources had an effect on where your town or city was started. Then, find out what renewable energy sources are still being used today. Make a chart of "Past Uses" and "Future Uses." How have they changed? How are they the same? Could they influence how your town grows and changes in the future.

Old factory in New York

Sum It Up

Where you get the energy to do day-to-day work will depend on decisions you make in the future. There are benefits and costs to any choice made concerning energy use. Some of the factors that have to be weighed when making energy choices include the present and future costs in time, money, and safety of a given energy source, the location where it's needed, and its ecological impact.

Critical Thinking

1. If you lived near a water source, what would be the benefits of a hydroelectric plant built near you? What would be the disadvantages?
2. What would you have to consider if you were designing a solar energy collector for campers and backpackers?
3. Is wind a good source of energy for home use for day-to-day things like TV, radio, dishwasher, etc.? Why or why not?

Harbor at Savannah, Georgia

Solar collectors in Hawaii

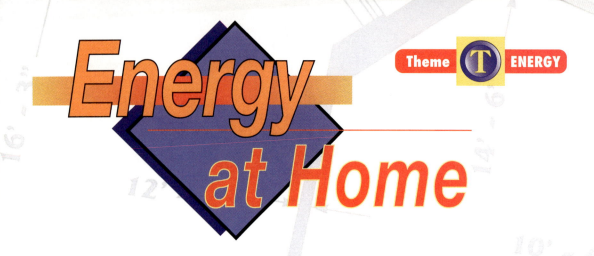

Energy at Home

Theme T ENERGY

There is a limited amount of fuel available to us, although some fuels are more plentiful than others. There are advantages and disadvantages with each renewable and nonrenewable energy source we use. We have to examine all the options and make responsible decisions for ourselves and for future generations.

Use everything you've learned about energy in this unit to design a home. Based on where the home will be, you need to decide how to heat and cool it, how much insulation to use, what energy sources you'll use, and what the land around the home will look like. Consider the energy needs of every room in your home. You may want to build a model of it, too. Be prepared to explain why you made the choices you did.

Wood stove

Underground home

Don't forget that some uses of renewable energy are simple and inexpensive. The Pueblo tribe of Native Americans used energy from the sun to heat their homes. Their homes were built with thick walls that absorbed the sun's heat during the day. The thick walls kept the inside of the home cool in the day, and the stored heat warmed their homes at night.

Installing fiberglass insulation

Literature Link
Facts on Water, Wind and Solar Power

Use *Facts on Water, Wind and Solar Power* by Guy Arnold to find out what renewable energy sources could be used or developed near where you live. Remember to consider the costs and benefits of renewable and nonrenewable energy sources when you design your home.

Using Energy To Get the Job Done

Everything we do is possible because of energy. We use energy to cook our food, to light and heat our homes, to move us from one place to another, and to operate our businesses and factories.

We need to use the energy sources that we have wisely, so that we don't waste them. We need to develop energy sources that haven't been used so that we are guaranteed abundant and affordable energy to do work for us for generations to come.

Minds On! How many uses of kinetic energy do you see at work in this picture? How many uses of potential energy do you see?

GLOSSARY

Use the pronunciation key below to help you decode, or read, the pronunciations.

Pronunciation Key

a	at, bad		d	dear, soda, bad
ā	ape, pain, day, break		f	five, defend, leaf, off, cough, elephant
ä	father, car, heart		g	game, ago, fog, egg
âr	care, pair, bear, their, where		h	hat, ahead
e	end, pet, said, heaven, friend		hw	white, whether, which
ē	equal, me, feet, team, piece, key		j	joke, enjoy, gem, page, edge
i	it, big, English, hymn		k	kite, bakery, seek, tack, cat
ī	ice, fine, lie, my		l	lid, sailor, feel, ball, allow
îr	ear, deer, here, pierce		m	man, family, dream
o	odd, hot, watch		n	not, final, pan, knife
ō	old, oat, toe, low		ng	long, singer, pink
ô	coffee, all, taught, law, fought		p	pail, repair, soap, happy
ôr	order, fork, horse, story, pour		r	ride, parent, wear, more, marry
oi	oil, toy		s	sit, aside, pets, cent, pass
ou	out, now		sh	shoe, washer, fish mission, nation
u	up, mud, love, double		t	tag, pretend, fat, button, dressed
ū	use, mule, cue, feud, few		th	thin, panther, both
ü	rule, true, food		<u>th</u>	this, mother, smooth
ů	put, wood, should		v	very, favor, wave
ûr	burn, hurry, term, bird, word, courage		w	wet, weather, reward
ə	about, taken, pencil, lemon, circus		y	yes, onion
b	bat, above, job		z	zoo, lazy, jazz, rose, dogs, houses
ch	chin, such, match		zh	vision, treasure, seizure

biomass (bī′ ō mas′) any once living material

calorie (kal′ ə rē) the amount of heat required to raise one gram of liquid water at standard pressure one degree Celsius

Celsius, Anders (sel′ sē əs) (1701–1744) Swedish scientist famous for the temperature scale which bears his name

Celsius scale (sel′ sē əs skāl) metric temperature scale with 100 degrees separating 0°C, the freezing point of water, and 100°C, the boiling point of water

chemical compounds (kem′ i kəl kom′ poundz) combinations of chemical elements with properties different from their component parts

chemical potential energy (kem′ i kəl pō ten′ shəl) the energy stored in chemical bonds when elements combine to form compounds

conduction (kən duk′ shən) transfer of thermal energy from particle to particle, most effective in solids

convection (kən vek′ shən) transfer of heat in liquid and gases by currents of rising, less dense material

data (dāt′ ə) information

electric energy (i lek′ trik) the kinetic energy of moving electrons produced either by generators or electric cells

energy the ability to do work

Fahrenheit, Gabriel Daniel (far′ ən hīt′) German scientist famous for the temperature scale that bears his name

Fahrenheit scale temperature scale with 180 degrees between the freezing point of water, 32°F, and the boiling point of water, 212°F

fiberglass (fī′ bər glas′) durable, nonflammable material made of fine threads of glass used for insulation, textiles, and many other purposes

fossil fuels (fos′ əl fū′ əlz) carbon-rich fuels formed from the remains of ancient animals and plants. Coal, oil, and natural gas are all fossil fuels.

friction (frik′ shən) force that resists motion between two objects in contact

geothermal energy (jē′ ō thur′ məl) energy from the heat inside Earth, usually carried to the surface by superheated water and steam

geyser (gī′ zər) a natural hot spring that shoots hot water and steam into the air after they're heated by hot rocks in the ground

heat thermal energy traveling from one place to another

homeostasis (hō′ mē ō stā′ sis) a delicate balance between many things. In the human body, the balance among many heating and cooling mechanisms

hydroelectric (hī′ drō i lek′ trik) electric power obtained by using the kinetic energy of falling water to operate a generator

hypothesis (hī poth′ ə sis) an unproved, temporary explanation based on known facts that can be used as a basis for further experimentation or investigation

insulators (in′ sə lā′ tərz) materials which do not transmit thermal energy well

kilocalorie (kil′ ə kal′ ə rē) or 1,000 calories, often written Calories. Most often used to measure energy in food

kinetic energy (ki net′ ik) the energy of objects in motion

mechanical energy (mi kan′ i kəl) is the energy of moving objects

mercury (mûr′ kyə rē) a dense, silvery, poisonous metallic element. The only metallic element that is a liquid at room temperature.

nonrenewable (non′ ri nü′ ə bəl) for energy, a source that can't be replaced by natural means in any time less than 30 years.

nuclear energy (nü klē ər) the energy produced by splitting atoms of transuranic elements, usually uranium or plutonium

pacemaker (pās′ mā′ kər) a medical device that helps patients with heart arrhythmia. It works by triggering heartbeats with small electric pulses directly to the heart muscle.

piston (pis′ tən) the part of an engine that is moved in the cylinder by expanding gases

potential energy (pə ten′ shəl) the energy something has because of where it is, its shape, or its condition

radiation (rā′ dē ā′ shən) a way of transferring heat by electromagnetic waves that requires no intervening matter

renewable (ri nü′ ə bəl) for energy, a source that can be replaced by natural means in less than 30 years

science an orderly way of thought and investigation for finding reliable information about how the physical world functions

scientific method (sī′ ən tif′ ik meth′ əd) any one of several orderly methods for testing information about the world for reliability

temperature (tem′ pər ə chər) the average thermal energy of particles in matter.

thermal energy (thûr′ məl) the total internal kinetic and potential energy from the random motion of particles in matter

thermostat (thûr′ mə stat′) a device to control temperature that uses some form of thermometer to open and close a switch

turbines (tûr′ bīnz) fan-like devices that transform the kinetic energy of moving fluids to the rotary motion of a shaft

ultraviolet light (ul′ trə vī′ ə lit) high-energy, non-visible light which can damage skin cells and lead to skin cancer, also responsible for tanning

vacuum (vak′ ūm) a space completely empty of matter

vacuum bottle (vak′ ūm bot′ əl) a glass or steel bottle consisting of two layers of material with a near vacuum in between them. Most often used to keep liquids hot or cool.

INDEX

Antarctica, 64–65
Arnold, Guy, 13, 81
Atoms, 60–61, 65; *illus.,* 61; nucleus of, 60–61; *illus.,* 61; and thermal energy, 61; *illus.,* 61

Beyond the Door **(Blackwood),** 12, 56
Biomass, 77
Blackwood, Gary, 12
Book reviews, 12–13

Calories, 32
Car engines: motion of, 54; *illus.,* 54
Celsius, Anders, 35
Celsius scale, 35; *act.,* 35; *illus.,* 34
Chemical potential energy, 21, 23, 25, 54, 57–58; *act.,* 21; *illus.,* 21
Chernobyl, 61
Coal, 58–59, 62; *illus.,* 58–59
Coal burning power plant, 56–57; *illus.,* 56–57
Cobb, Vickie, 13
Conduction, 42, 45, 49; *illus.,* 42
Conservation, 62–63; *act.,* 63; of fossil fuels, 62–65
Convection, 43, 45, 49; *act.,* 43; *illus.,* 43; and wind, 70

Dams, 74; *illus.,* 74
Data, 9; *act.,* 10

Earth-heat energy, 76

Electric energy, 57; *illus.,* 56–57
Electricity, 56–58; *illus.,* 56–57; and solar energy, 73
Energy auditor, 48
Energy: defined, 6

Facts on Water, Wind and Solar Power **(Arnold),** 13, 81
Fahrenheit, Gabriel Daniel, 34
Fahrenheit's scale, 34; *illus.,* 34, 52
Fiberglass, 47; *illus.,* 47
Fossil fuels, 58–65; *illus.,* 58–59; and Antarctica, 64–65; coal, 58–59; *illus.,* 59; conservation of, 62–63; *act.,* 63; costs of, 64; early use by the Chinese of, 60; *illus.,* 60; natural gas, 58–59; *illus.,* 58–59; oil, 58–59; *illus.,* 58–59; petroleum, 58–59; *illus.,* 58–59; and pollution, 61, 64
Friction, 20; *illus.,* 20

Geothermal energy, 76
Geysers, 76; *illus.,* 76

Heat, 20, 26–37; *act.,* 28–29; and calories, 32; and thermal energy, 32–33; transfer of, 38–49; traveling of, 38–39
Heat absorption: by colors, 48–49; *act.,* 48

Home design: and energy, 80–81
Homeostasis, 36
Hot springs, 76
How to Think Like a Scientist **(Kramer),** 13
Hydroelectric plants, 74
Hydroelectric power, 74
Hypothesis, 9; *act.,* 10

Insulation, 47–48; *illus.,* 47; and insulators, 47
Insulators, 47

Jacobs, Linda, 13

Kinetic energy, 14–20, 22, 25, 30, 54, 57, 82–83; *act.,* 16–17; *illus.,* 19, 82–83
Kramer, Stephen, P., 13

Letting Off Steam **(Jacobs),** 13
Literature: in science, 12–13

MacGregor, Ellen, 13
Manure: as energy source, 77
Mechanical energy, 54
Miss Pickerell Tackles the Energy Crisis **(MacGregor and Pantell),** 13
Mercury, 34

Natural gas, 58–59, 62; *illus.,* 58–59
Nonrenewable energy sources, 58, 60, 62
Nuclear energy, 60–61;

and Chernobyl, 61; and nuclear generating plants, 61
Nuclear generating plants (nuclear power plants), 61
Nucleus, of atoms, 61

Oil, 58–59, 62; *illus.*, 58–59

Pantell, Dora, 13
Pacemaker, 23–24; *illus.*, 23
Pendulum, 22; *illus.*, 22
Petroleum, 58–59; *illus.*, 58–59
Piston, 54, 55; *illus.*, 54, 55
Pollution: from energy sources, 61, 64, 71, 74–77; and biomass, 77; and fossil fuels, 61, 64; and geothermal energy, 76; and hydroelectric plants, 74; and nuclear energy, 61; and solar energy, 72–73; and tidal generators, 75; and wind energy, 71
Potential energy, 18–25, 82–83; *act.*, 15, 16–17; *illus.*, 82–83; of atoms, 60; changes in form, 20; *act.*, 20

Radiation, 44–45, 49; *act.*, 44; *illus.*, 44–45
Renewable energy sources, 66–79, *act.*, 68–69; and the energy inside Earth, 70, 76; *illus.*, 76; and moving water, 70; and once–living matter, 70, 77; and the sun, 70, 72, 73; and wind, 70–71; and the water, 74; and the tides, 75

Scientific Method, 8–11; *act.*, 10
Solar collectors, 72, 73, *illus.*, 72, 73
Solar energy, 72–73; *act.*, 72; and electricity, 73; *illus.*, 72–73; and pollution, 72; and solar collectors, 73; and solar energy generators, 73; and wind, 70
Solar energy generators, 73
Sources of energy: location of, 78–79
Steam-driven factory, 56; *illus.*, 56
Steam engines, 55–56; *illus.*, 55, motion of, 55; *illus.*, 55

Temperature, 30; *act.*, 28–29; *illus.*, 30; and Celsius, 35; *illus.*, 35; and Fahrenheit, 34; *illus.*, 34; and homeostasis, 36; *illus.*, 36; measuring of, 34–37; and thermostats, 36
Thermal energy, 31, 37; *act.*, 31; *illus.*, 31; and atoms, 61; *illus.*, 61; and conduction, 42; *act.*, 40–41; *illus.*, 42; controlling transfer of, 46–49; *act*, 46; *illus.*, 47; and convection, 47; *illus.*, 47; and heat, 32–33; *act.*, 33; *illus.*, 32; and insulation, 47–48; *illus.*, 47; and mass, 31; and movement, 54–55; and radiation, 44–45; *act.*, 44
Thermal energy transfer: controlling, 46–49; *act.*, 46
Thermometer, 30, 34, 35; *illus.*, 34
Thermostats, 36; *illus.*, 36
Tidal energy, 75
Tidal generators, 75; *illus.*, 75
Turbines, 57, 70, 74; *illus.*, 57, 70, 74

Ultraviolet light (UV), 72

Water energy, 74
Waterwheels, 74
Why Doesn't the Sun Burn Out? **(Cobb),** 13
Wind energy, 70–71; and convection, 70; and pollution, 71; and solar energy, 70; wind-generating farms, 71; *illus.*, 71; windmills, 66–71; *illus.*, 66–67, 71; wind turbines, 70–71; *illus.*, 70, 71
Wind-generating farms, 71; *illus.*, 71
Windmills, 66–71; *illus.*, 66–67, 71
Wind turbines, 70–71; *illus.*, 70, 7

CREDITS

Photo Credits:
Cover, The Image Bank/Larry Keenan Associates; **1,** Photoedit; **2-3,** UNIPHOTO; **3,** (t) Studiohio/1991; (b) ©UNIPHOTO; **5,** K.S. Studio/1991; **6-7,** Stuart Westmorland/Tom Stack and Associates; **7,** (itr) ©RM International Photography/Richard Haynes; (ibl) H. Armstrong Roberts, Inc; **8,** ©Culver Pictures; **9-10,** ©K.S. Studio; **11,** ©UNIPHOTO; **12-13,** ©Studiohio; **14-17,** ©K.S. Studio; **18-19,** ©Manny Millan/Sports Illustrated; **20,** (c) H. Armstrong Roberts, Inc.; **21,** (b) ©K.S. Studio; **22,** (l) Comstock, Inc., (r) H. Armstrong Roberts, Inc.; **23,** ©K.S. Studio; **24,** (tr) ©Doug Martin; (b) ©K.S. Studio; **25,** (tr) ©George Anderson; (b) ©K.S. Studio; **26-27,** Bruce Coleman Inc./J.C. Carton; **28-29,** ©Studiohio; **30,** ©Henry Groskinsky/Peter Arnold, Inc.; **31,** ©Doug Martin; **32,** ©K.S. Studio; **33-35,** ©Brent Turner; **36,** (tr) ©Doug Martin, (br) ©K.S. Studio; **37,** ©Jan Halaska/Photo Researchers; **38-39,** ©Photoedit; **40-41,** ©Studiohio; **42,** (tr) ©George Anderson; **42,** (c) ©K.S. Studio; **43,** ©George Anderson; **44-45,** ©Bob Daemmrich/Stock Boston; **47,** (tr) ©Phototake; **48,** (tr) ©Doug Martin; **49,** (tr) ©Brent Turner; (br) ©RM International; **50-51,** Bruce Coleman, Inc./Cameron Davidson; **50,** (itr) Susan Van Etten/Photoedit; **51,** (itr) ©Jon F. Silla/Transparencies, Inc., (ibr) The Stock Market; **52-53,** ©Studiohio; **55,** (tr) ©J.R. Holland/Stock Boston; **56-57,** Bryon Augustin; **58,** ©Astrid-Hans Frieder Michier/Photo Researchers; **59,** (tr) Earth Scenes/Breck P. Kent; **61,** ©Dan McCoy/Rainbow Photo; **62-63,** ©Allen Green/Photo Researchers; **64-65,** ©K. Scholz/H. Armstrong Roberts, Inc.; **65,** (itr) ©E.R. Degginger; **66-67,** ©Dale E. Boyer/Photo Researchers; **66,** (il) ©John Elk/Stock Boston; **68-69,** ©K.S. Studios; **71,** Paul Conklin/Photedit; **72,** (tc) Peter Menzel/Stock Boston; **73,** (br) Tony Freeman/Photoedit; **74,** (bc) Comstock, Inc.; **76,** David Ball/The Stock Market; **77,** ©Dean Abramson Photography; **78,** (tc) ©FPG International, (bc) Vincee Streano/Tony Stone Worldwide/Chicago, Ltd.; **79,** ©P.M. Chock/Stock Boston; **80-81,** The Image Bank/Grant Faith; **80,** (i) Abarno/The Stock Market; **81,** (itl) ©R. Lloyd/H. Armstrong Roberts, Inc.; **81,** (ibr) ©E.R. Degginger; **82-83,** Nik Wheeler/Westlight.

Illustration Credits:
23, Gina Lapurga; **47, 54, 55, 56, 57, 70, 75,** Bill Boyer; **52, 68,** Bob Giuliani; **58, 59, 60,** Bill Singleton; **74,** John Edwards; **61,** James Shough